A DAY IN NYC

A PICTORIAL DIVERSION FOR TIMES OF WAITING

IMAGES FROM ATWOOD

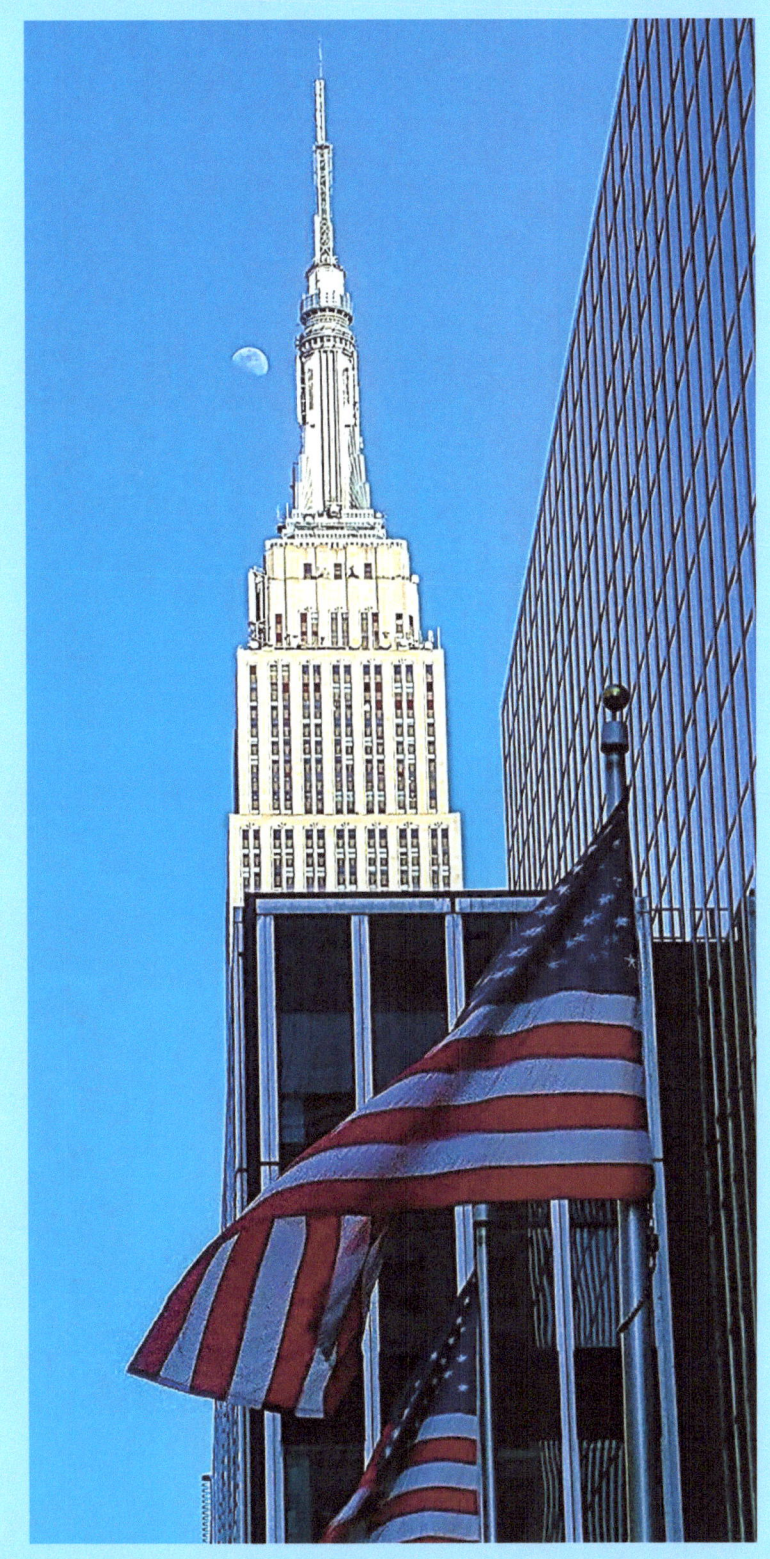

A DAY IN NYC
IMAGES FROM ATWOOD
A PICTORIAL DIVERSION FOR TIMES OF WAITING

COPYRIGHT 2017

ISBN : 978-0-9975819-6-6

Echo Hill Arts Press, LLC.
Colorado Springs, CO, USA

https://www.atwoodcutting.com
http://www.sleepigmoosesaga.com

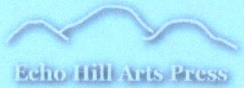

Echo Hill Arts Press

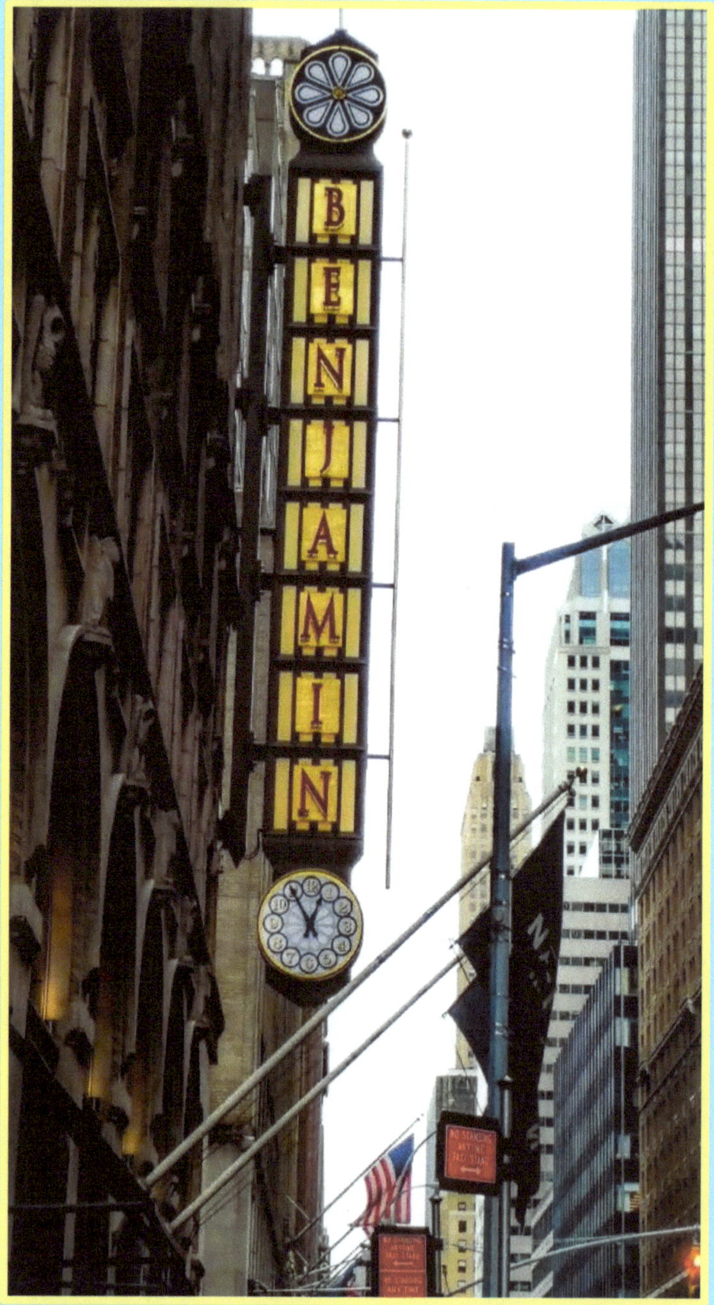

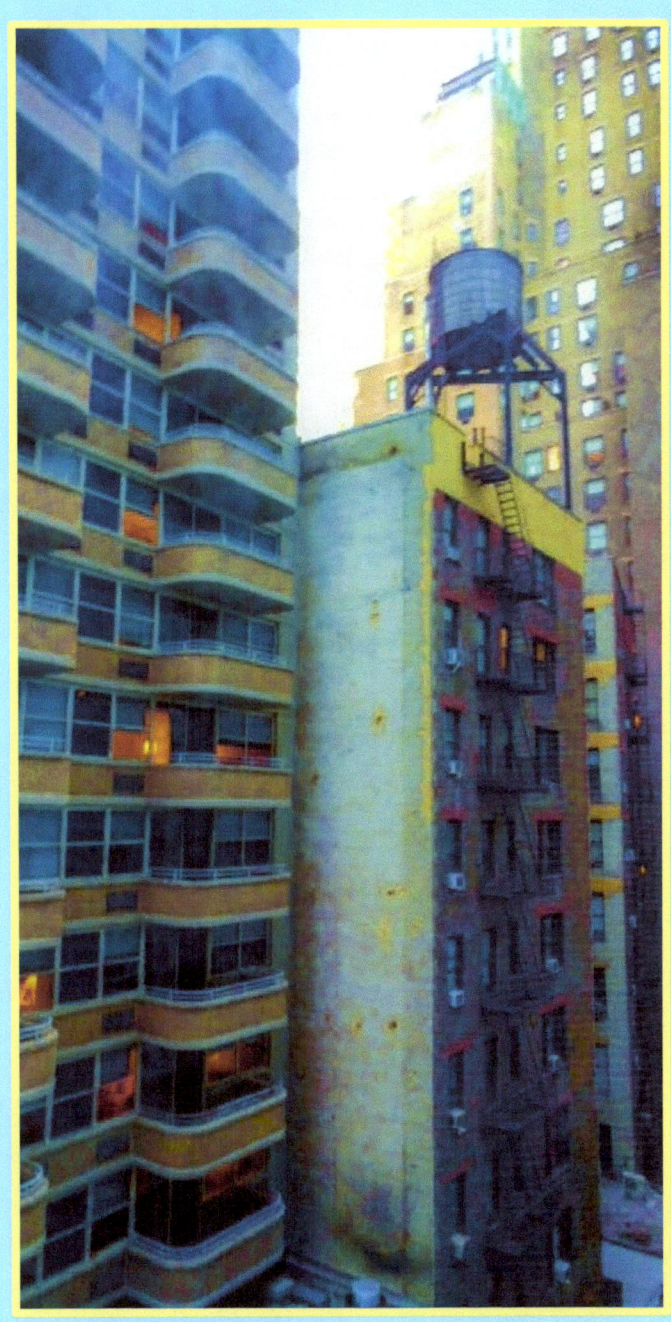

VENTURING
FROM
HER CABIN IN
THE WOODS
A VISITOR
BRAVES THE
BIG APPLE

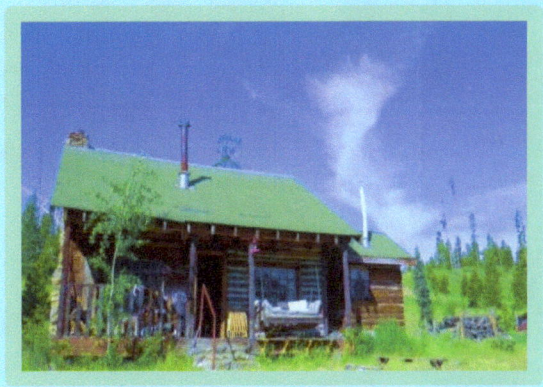

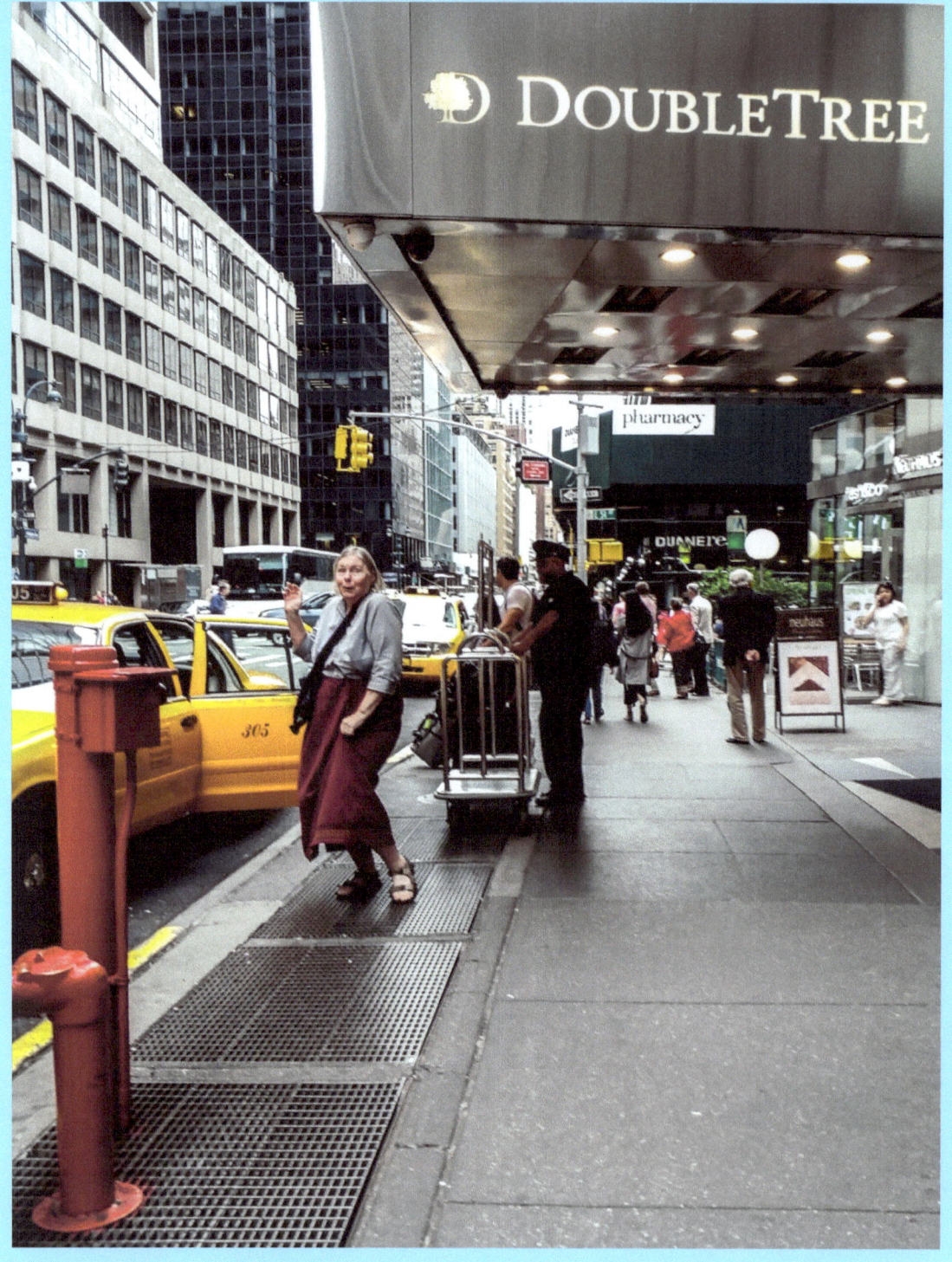

STARTING IN FRONT OF THE HILTON

POSING ON THE MARILYN MONROE GRATE

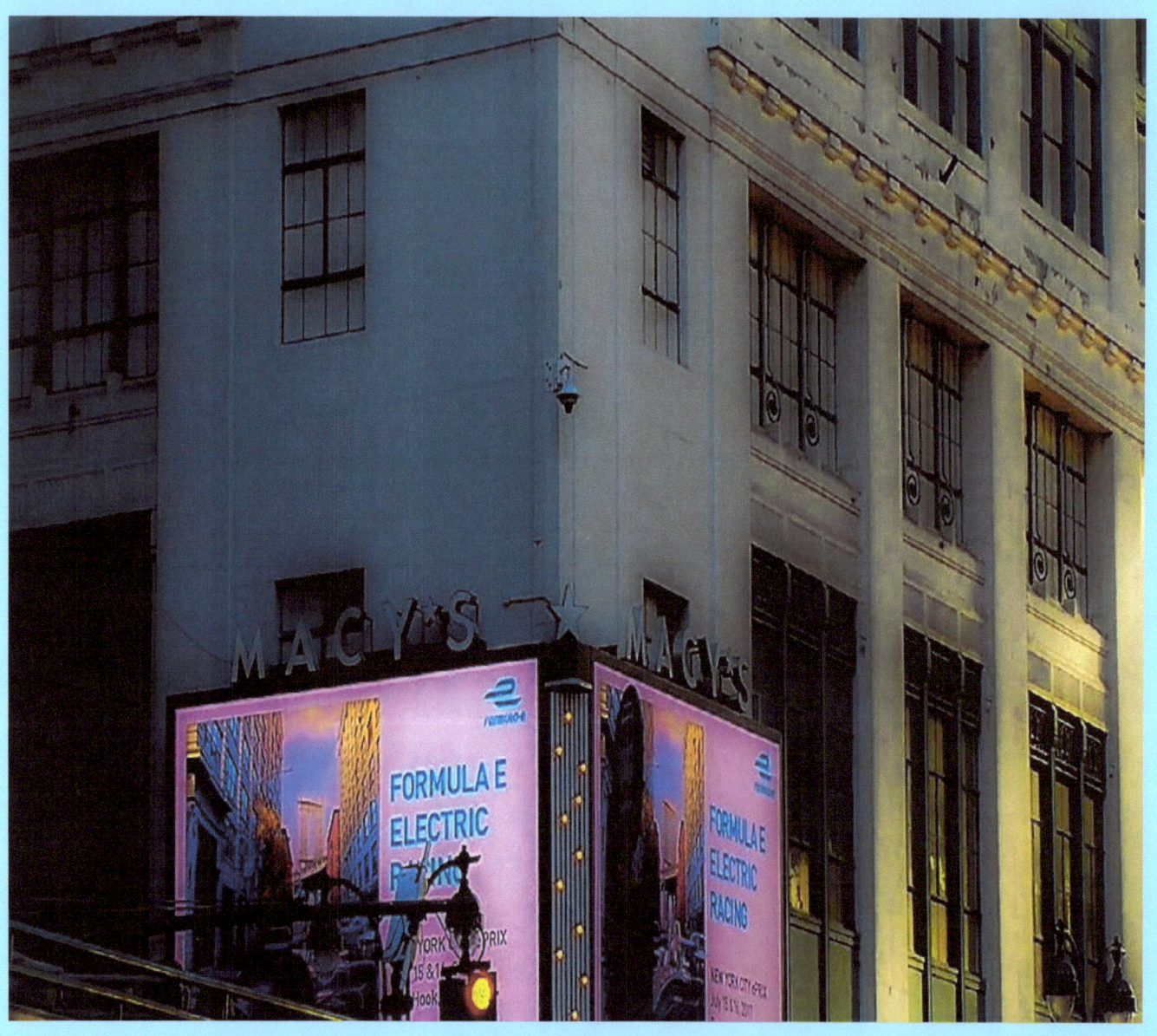

THERE'S AN ICON
ON EVERY CORNER

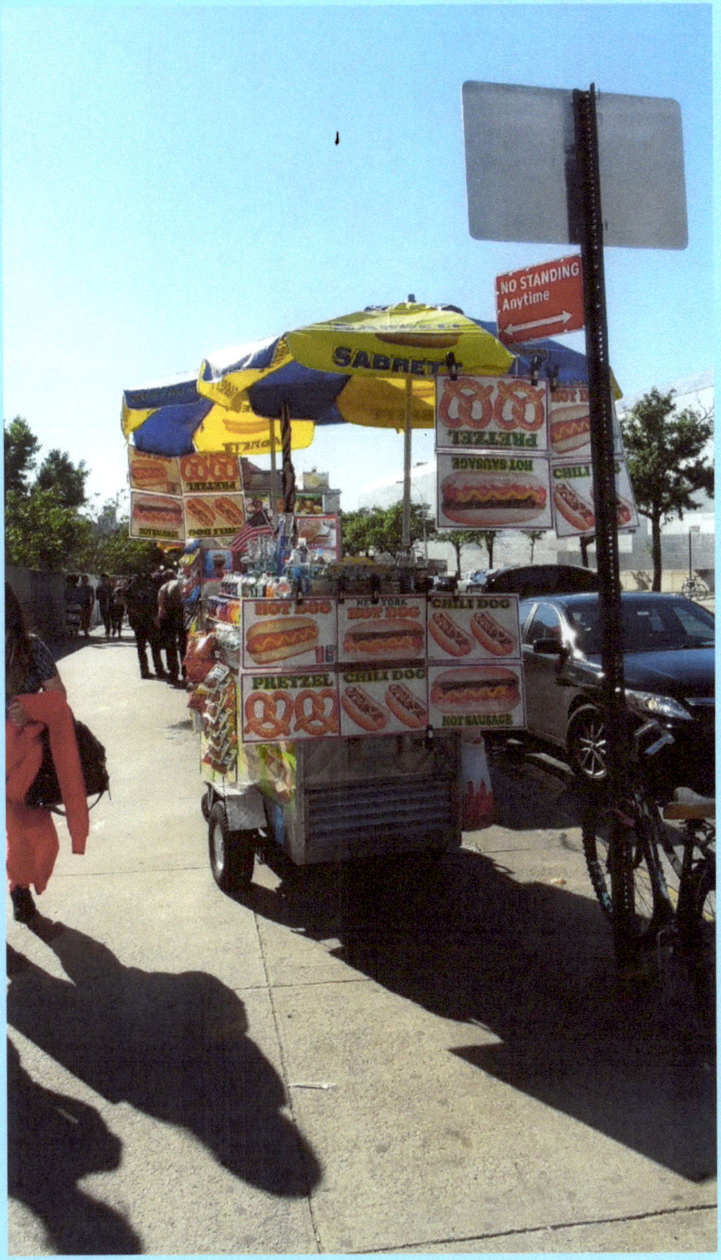

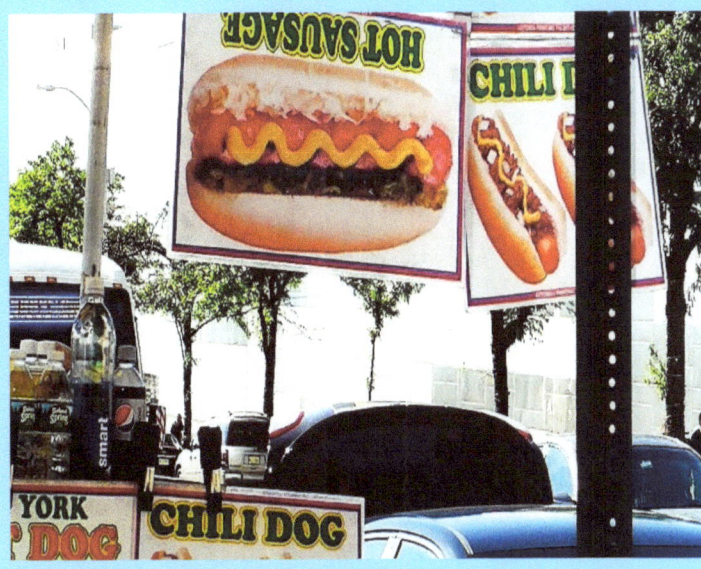

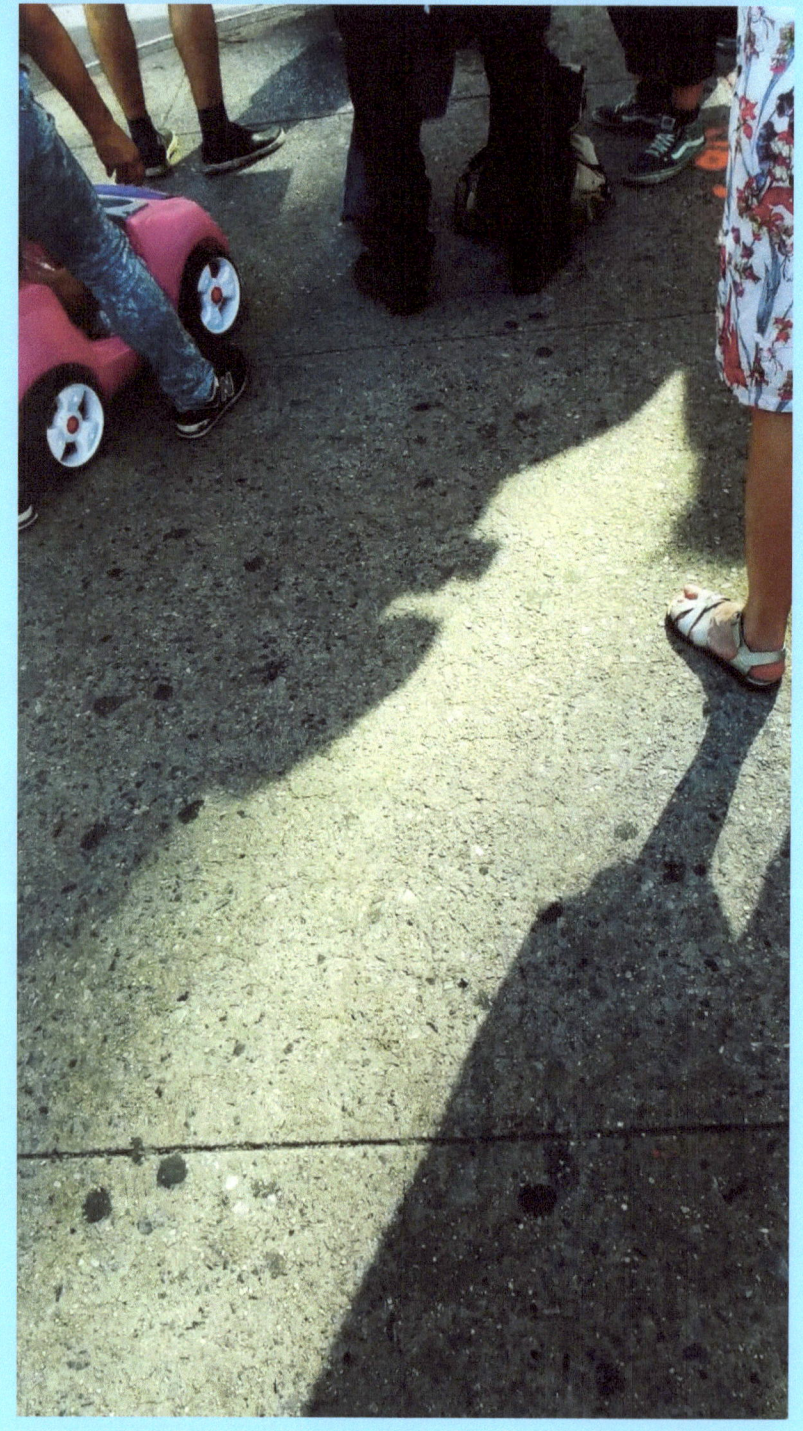

SHADOWS
OF

NEW
YORK

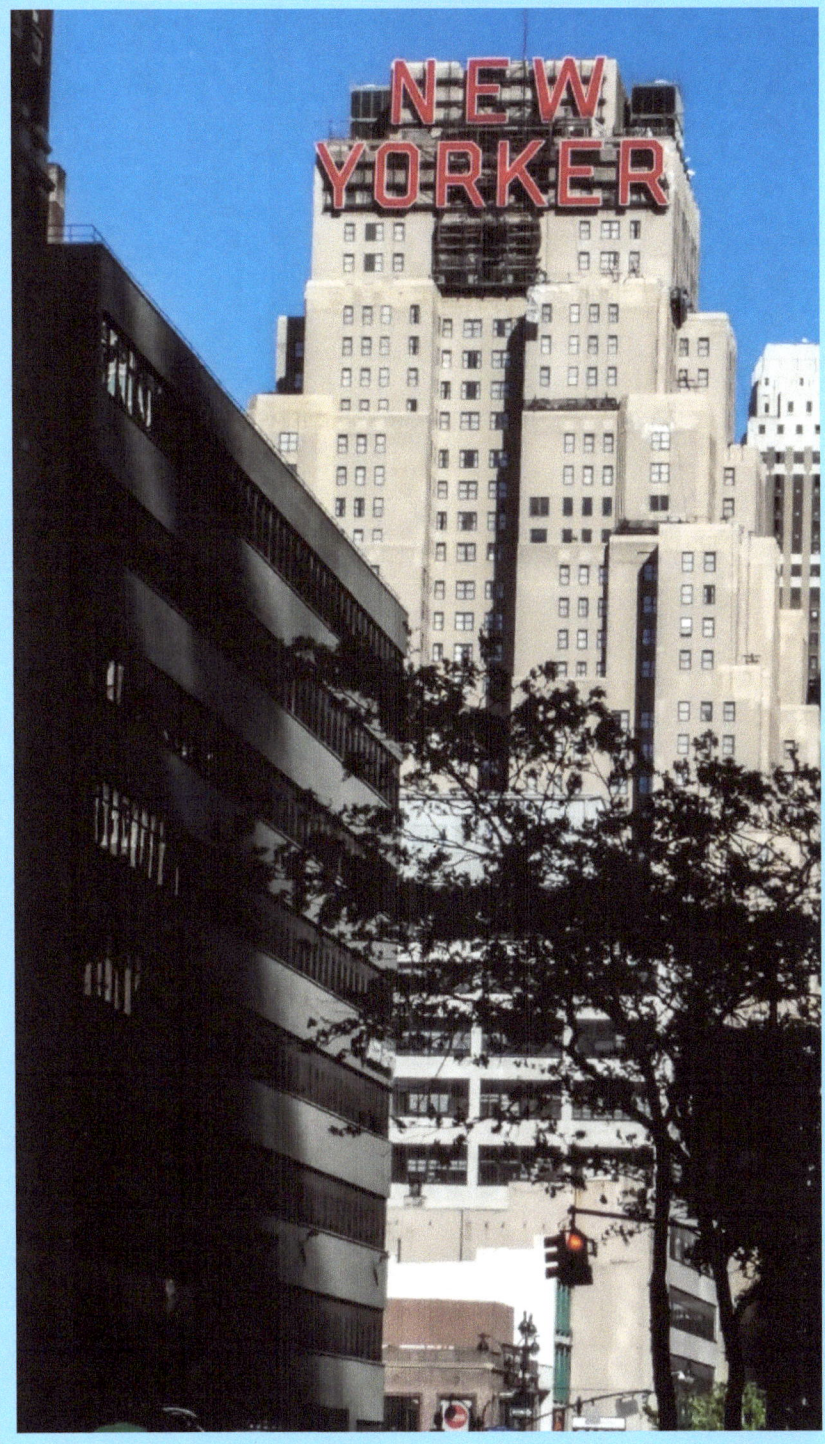

SHADOWS ON THE
NEW YORKER

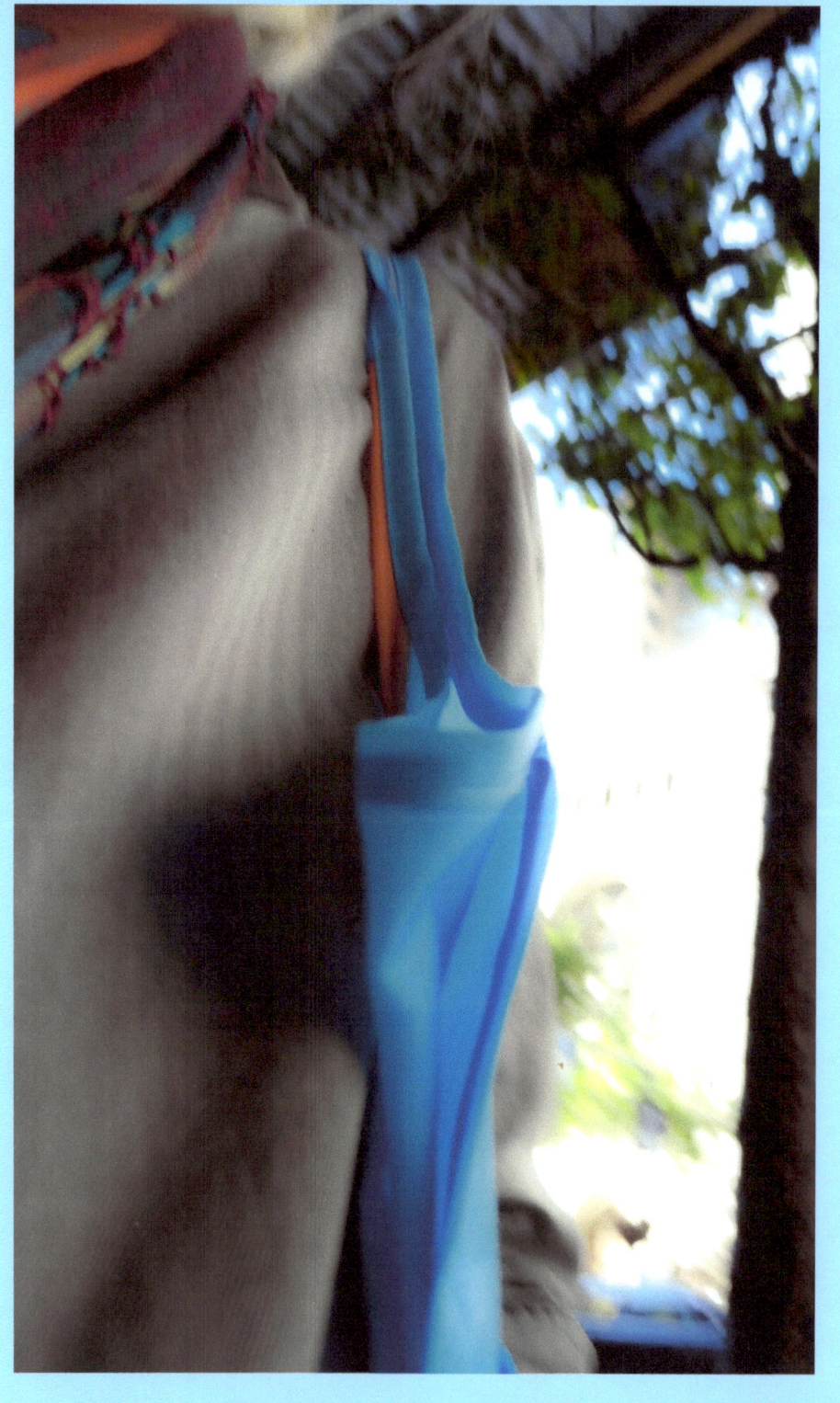

PATCHES

OF

LOCAL

COLOR

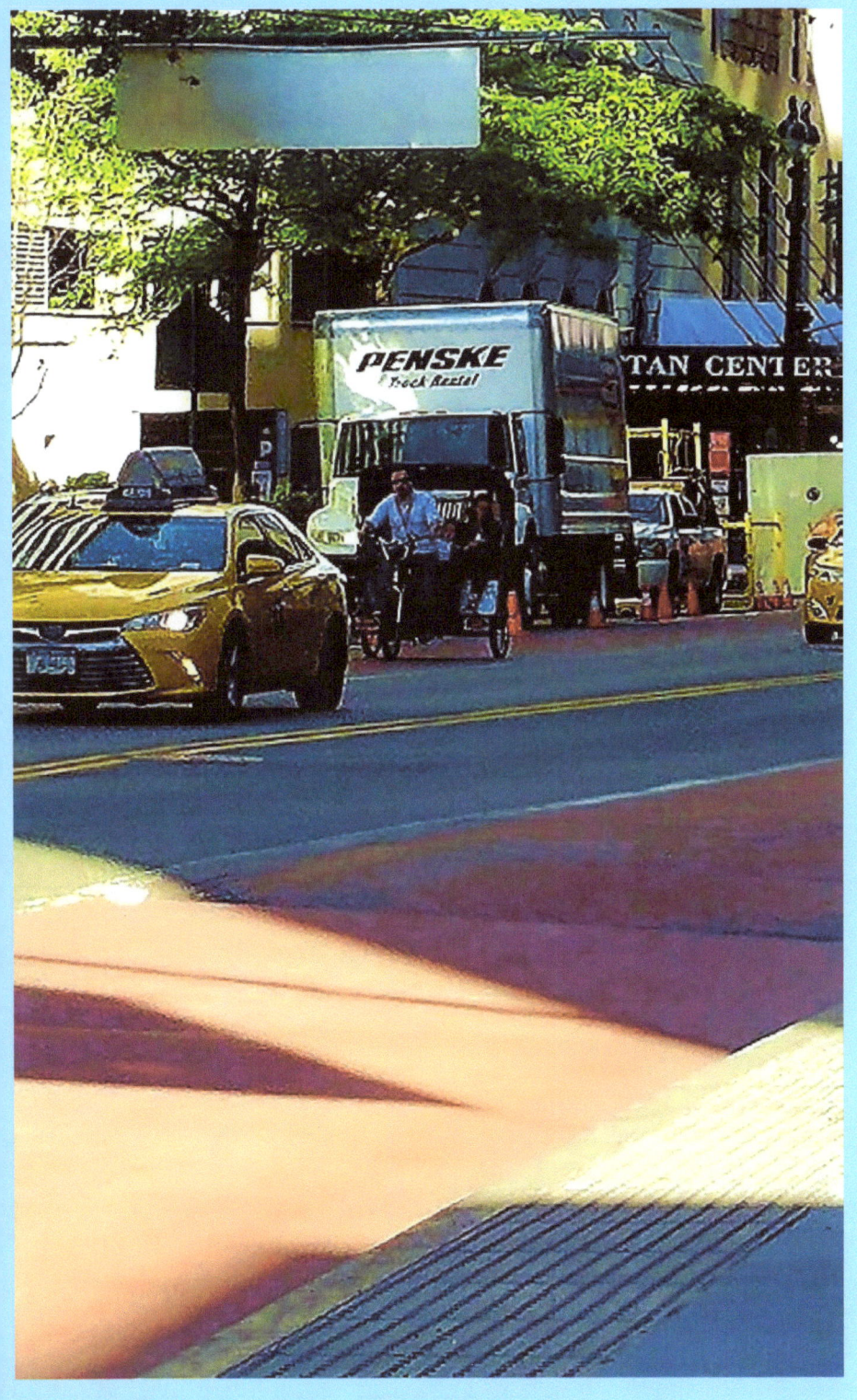

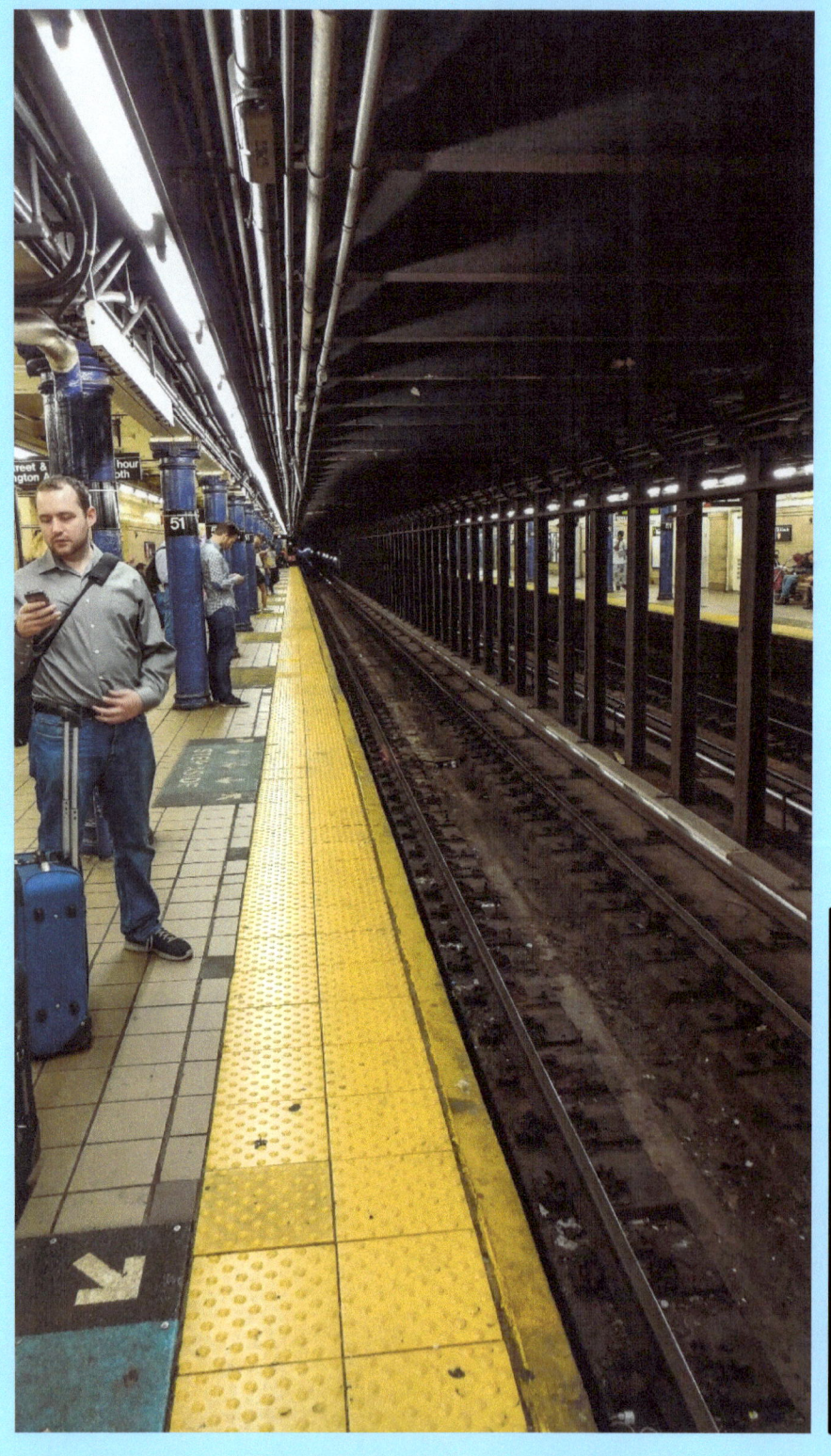

WAITING

BENEATH

51ST STREET

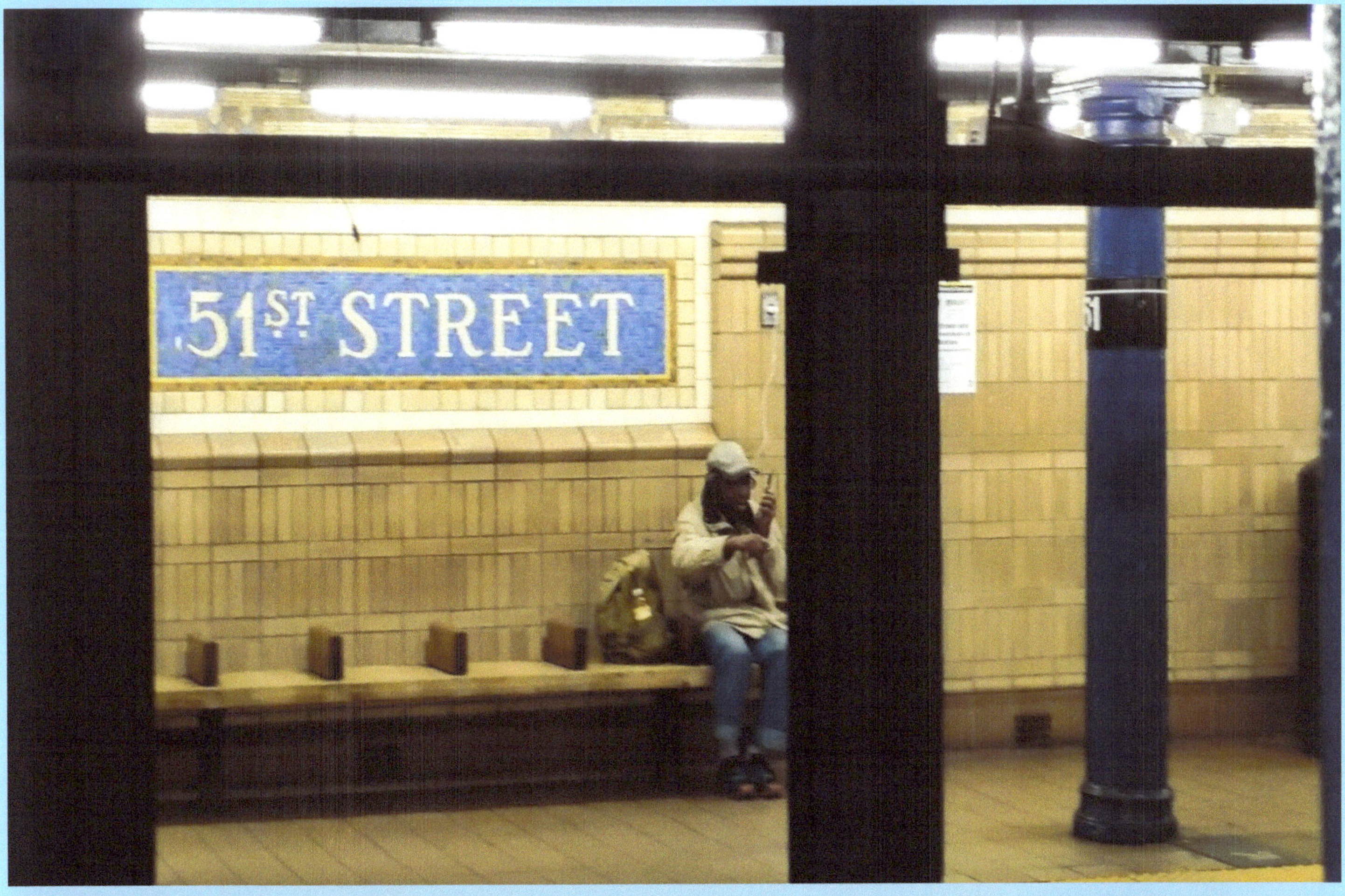

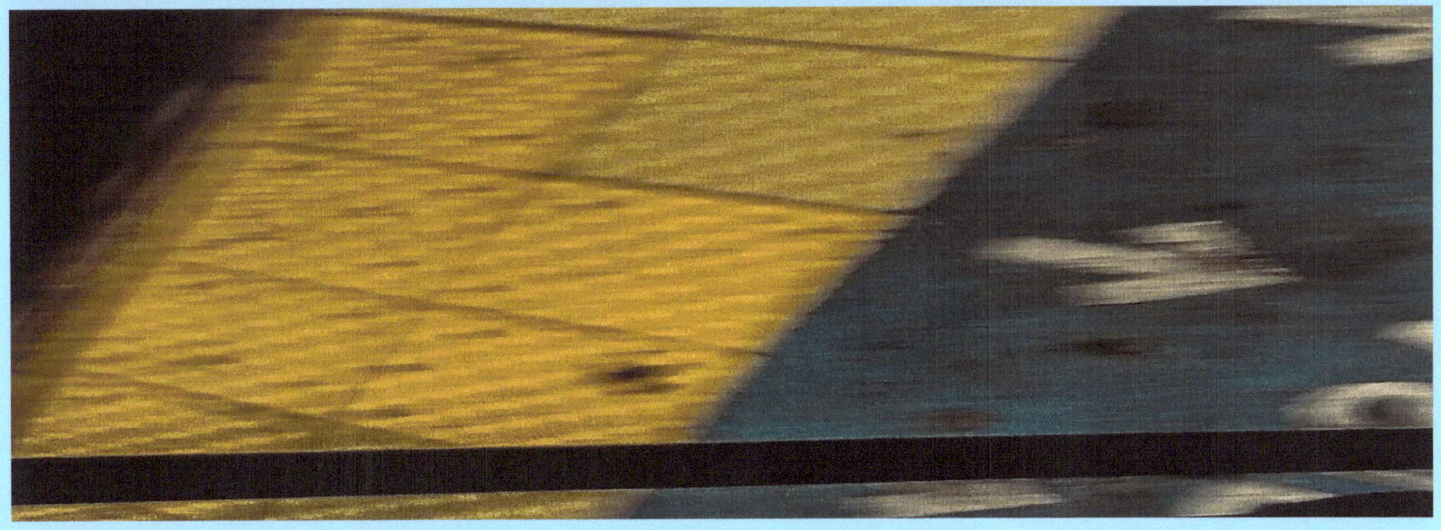

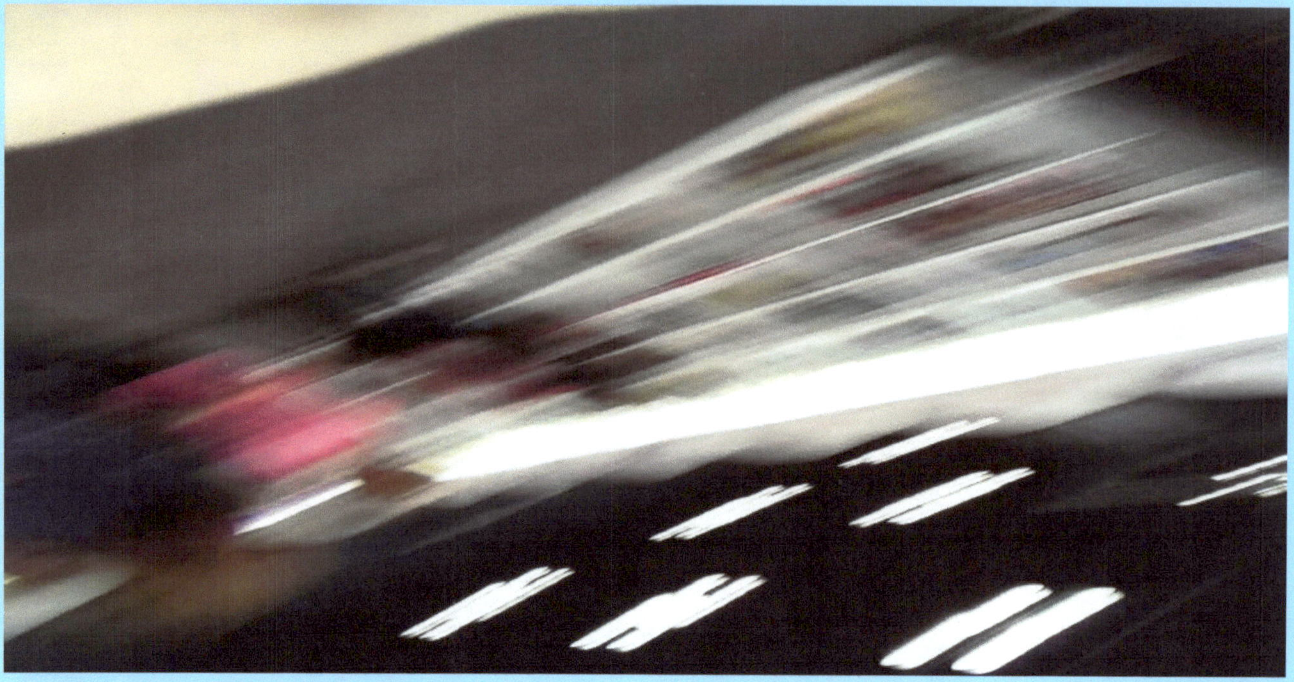

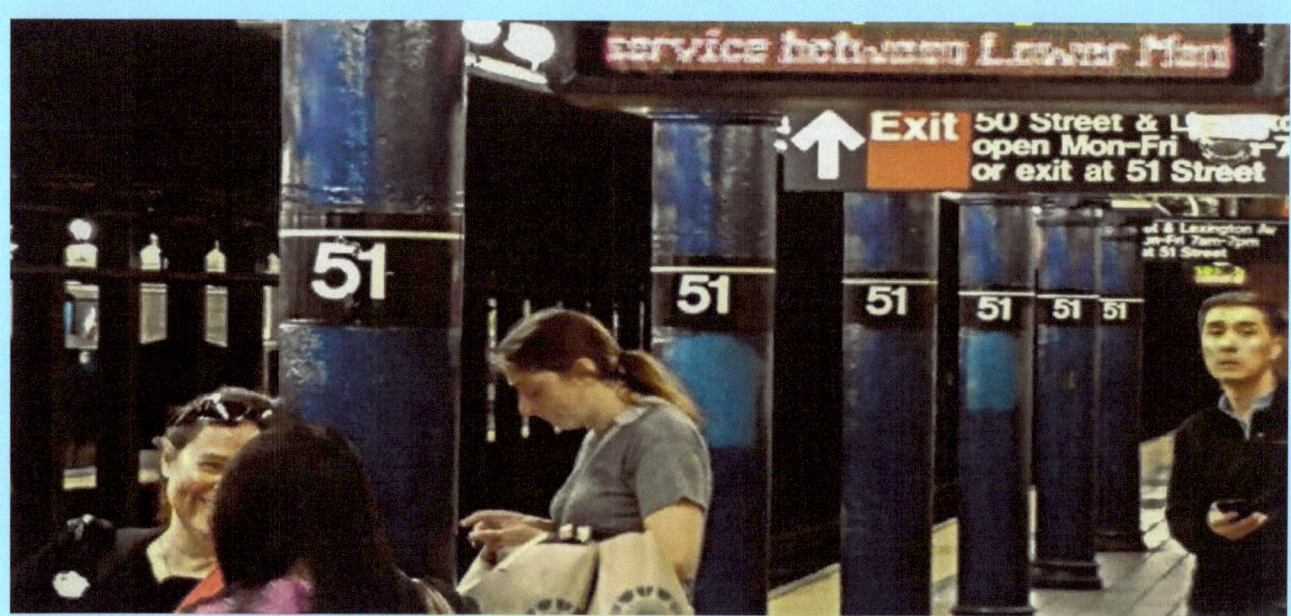

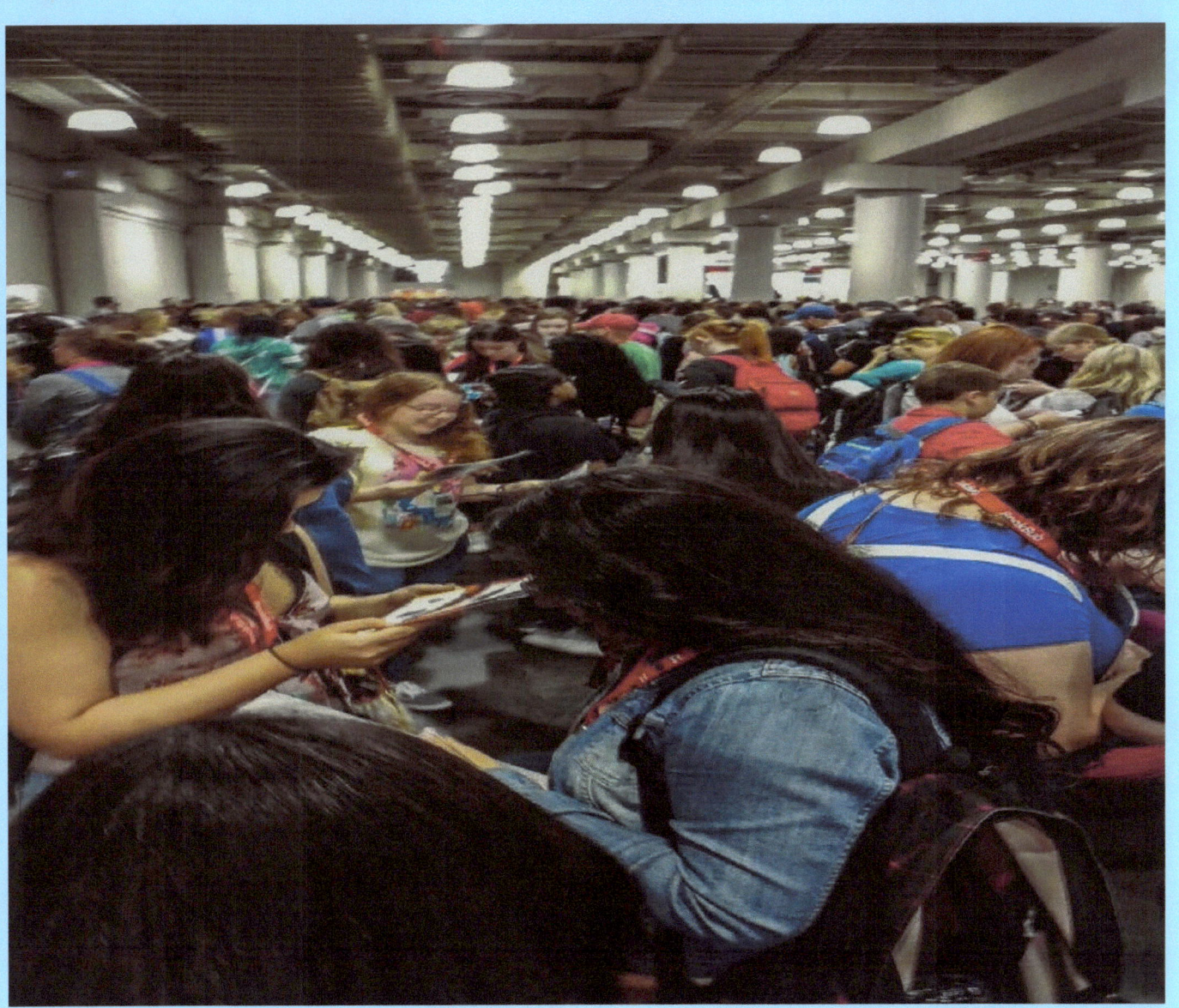

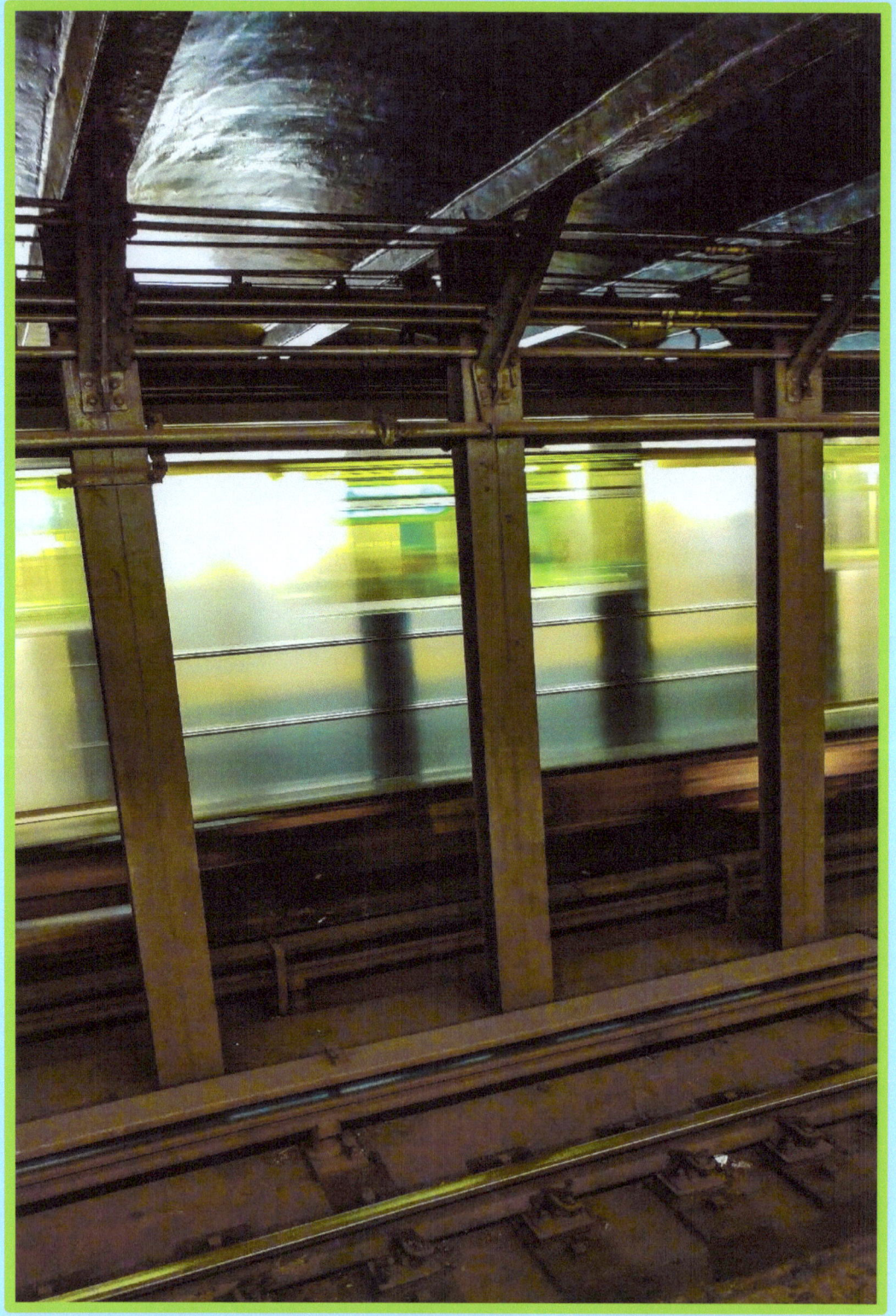

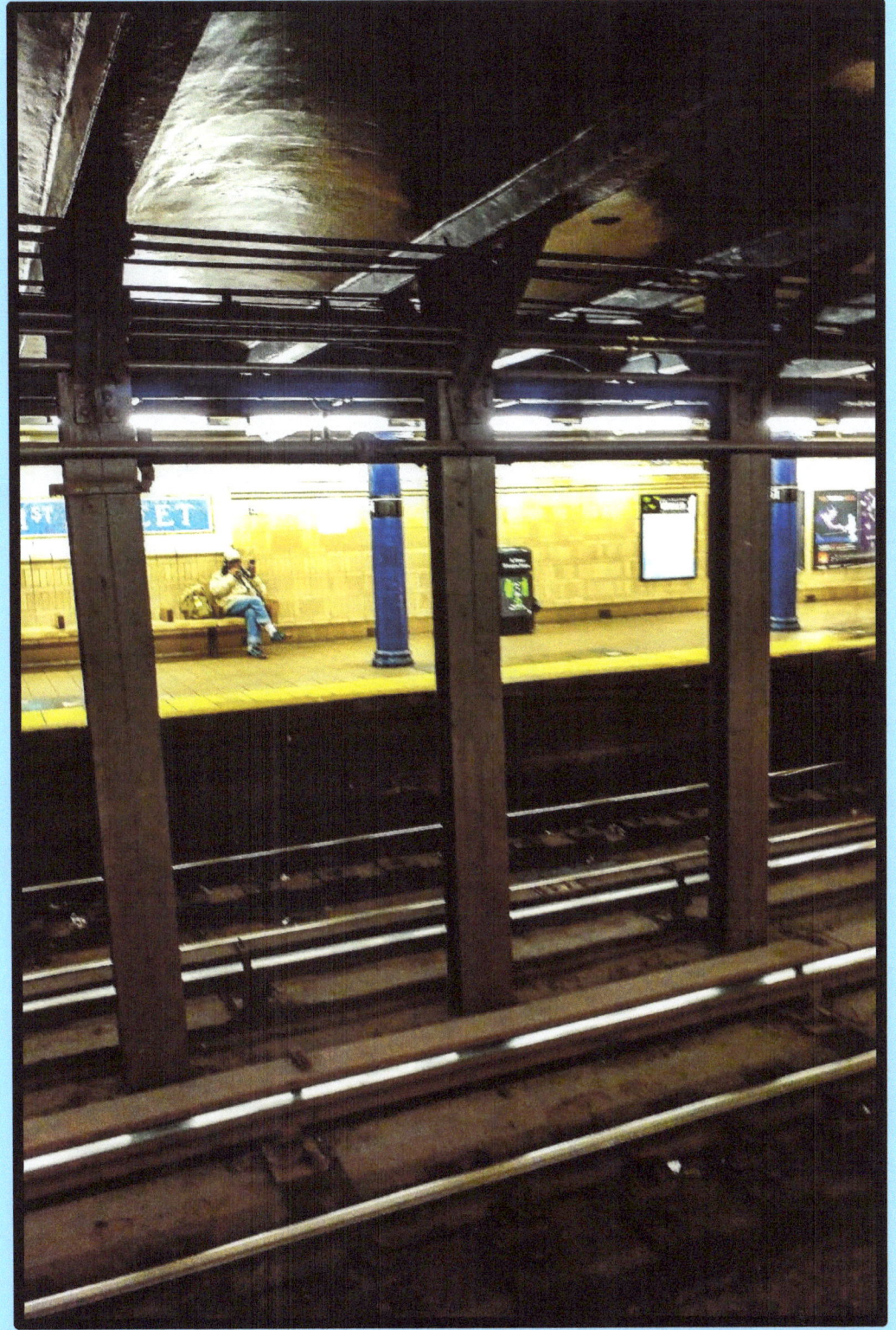

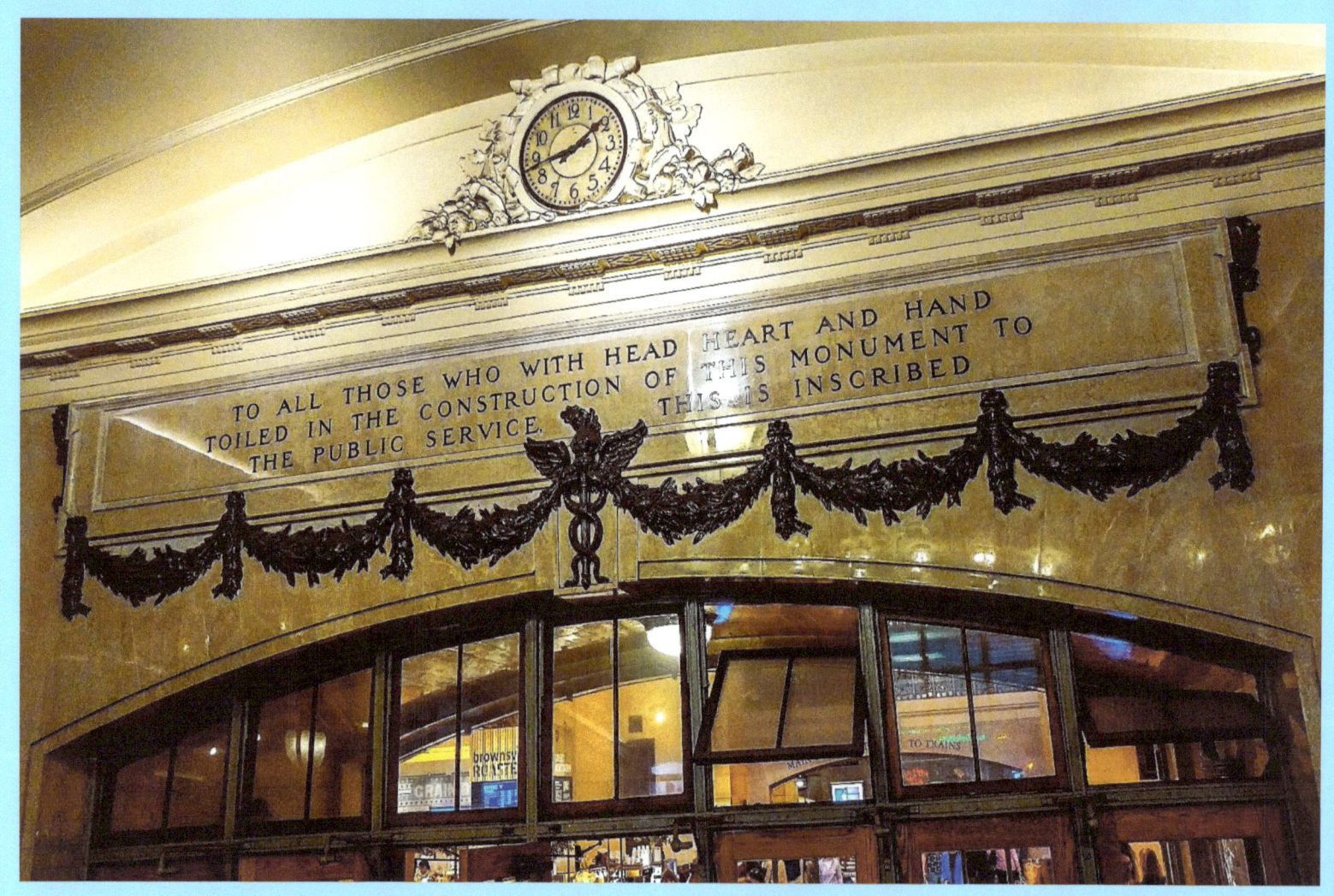

TO ALL THOSE WHO WITH HEAD HEART AND HAND TOILED IN THE CONSTRUCTION OF THIS MONUMENT TO THE PUBLIC SERVICE. THIS IS INSCRIBED

ON TO
GRAND CENTRAL STATION

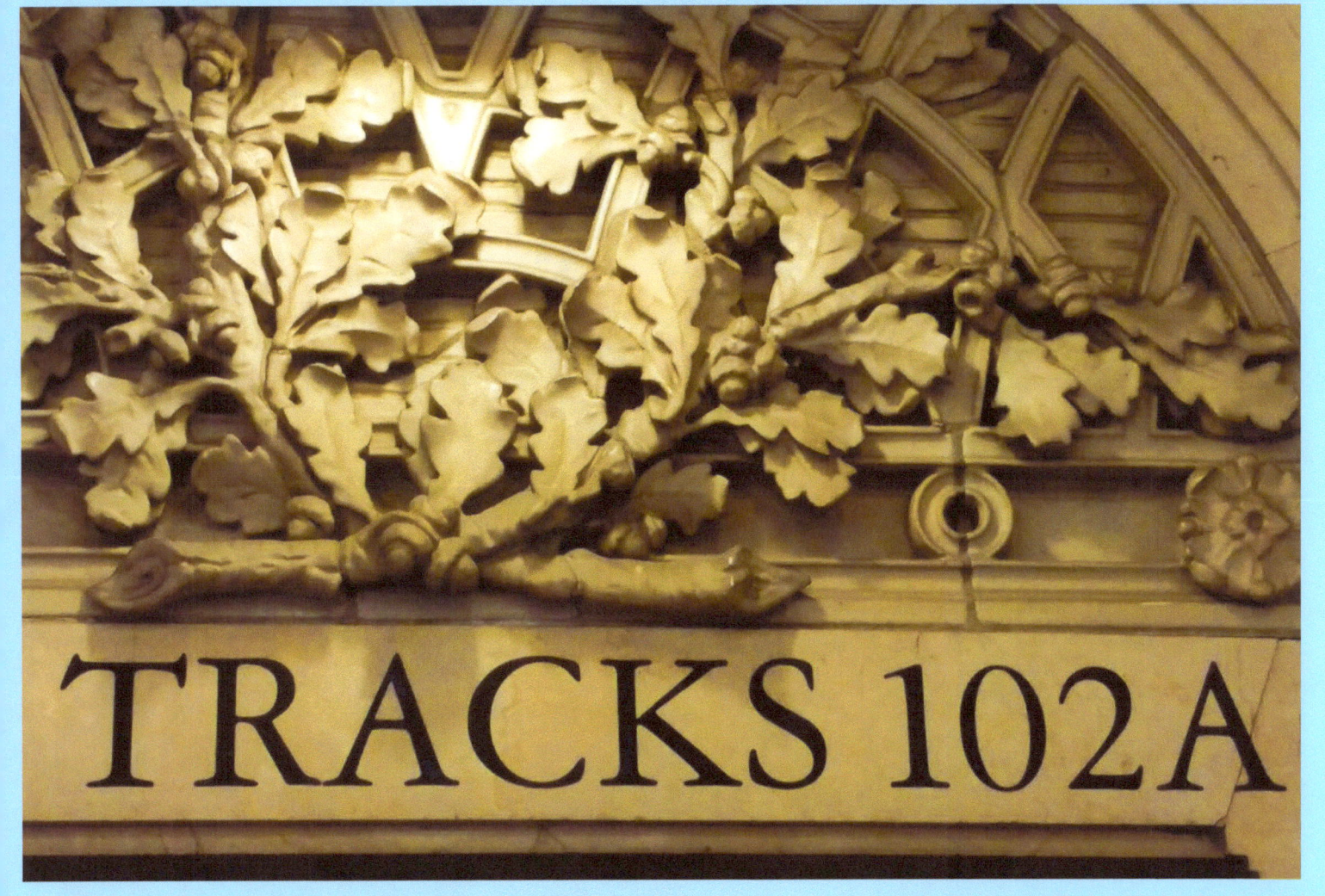

TRACKS 102A

FOR AN ARCHITECTURAL TREASURE HUNT

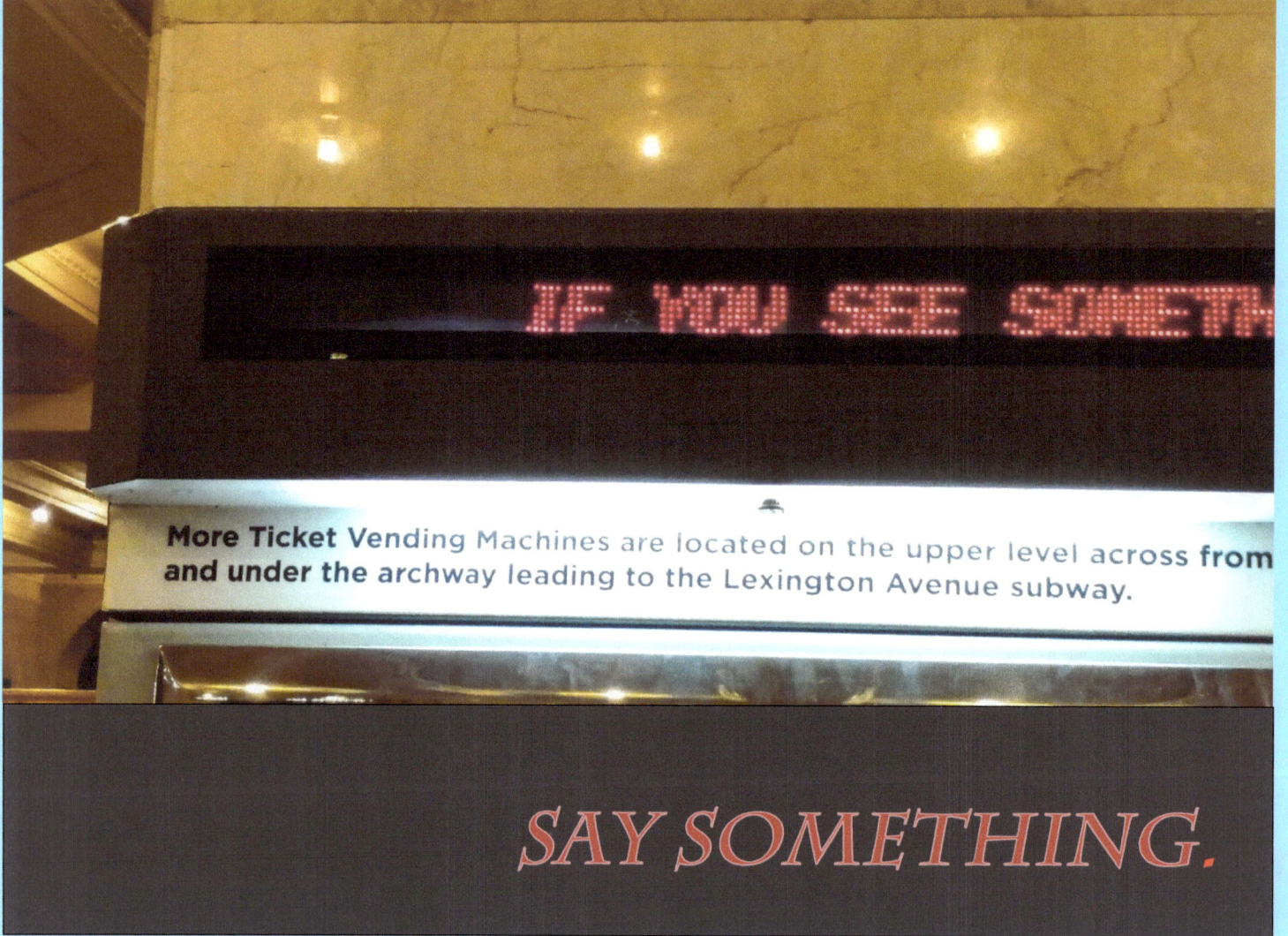

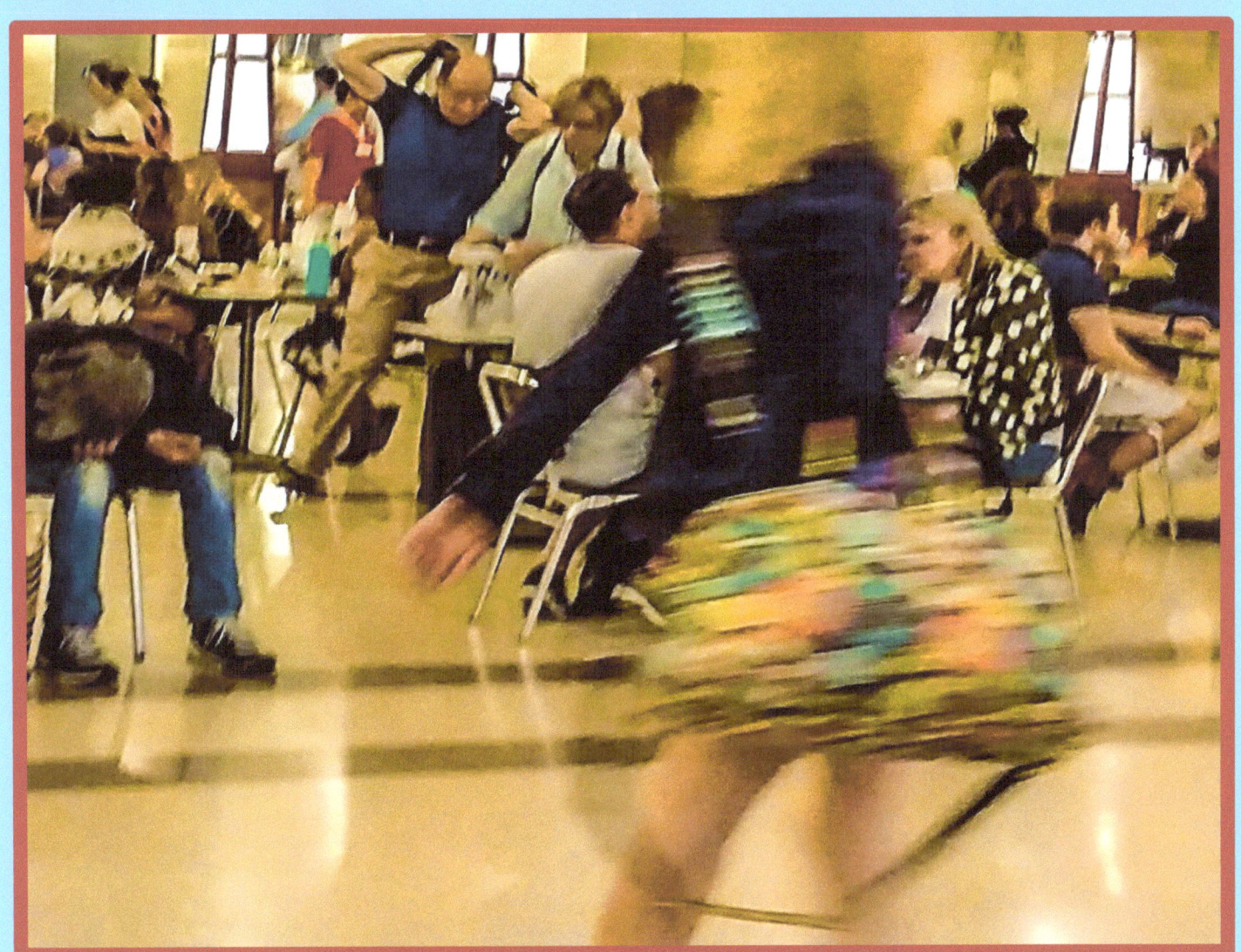

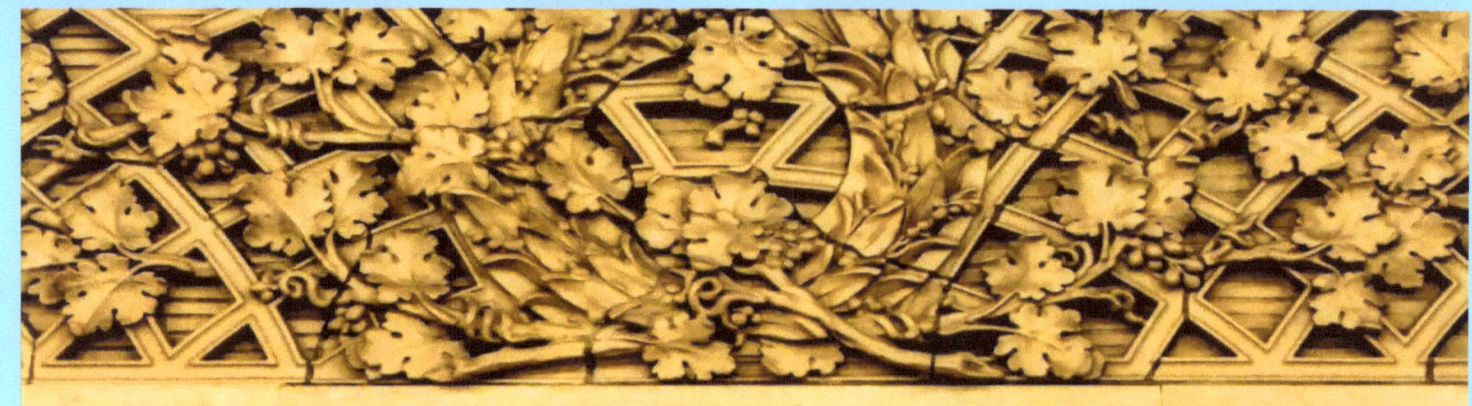

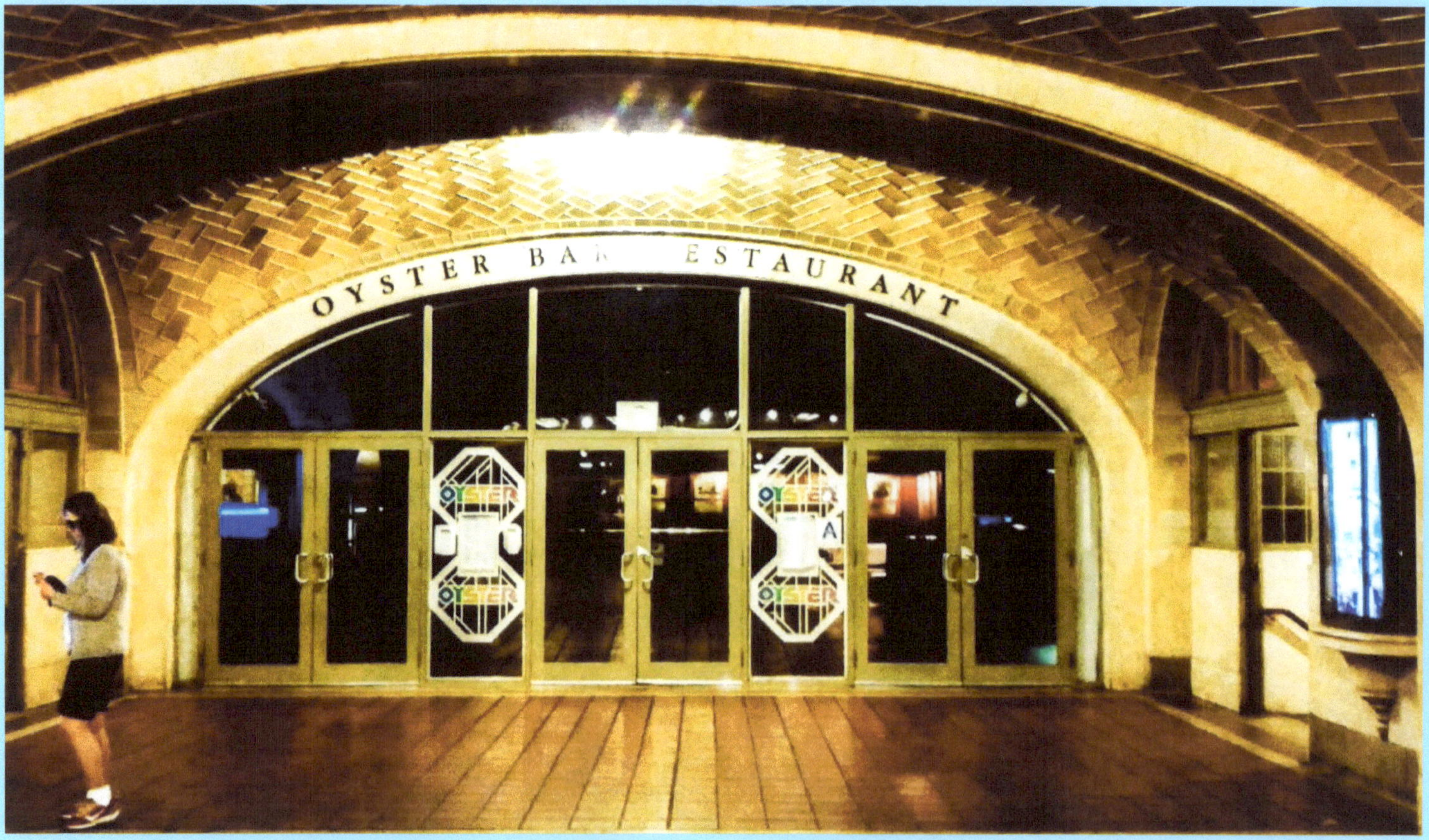

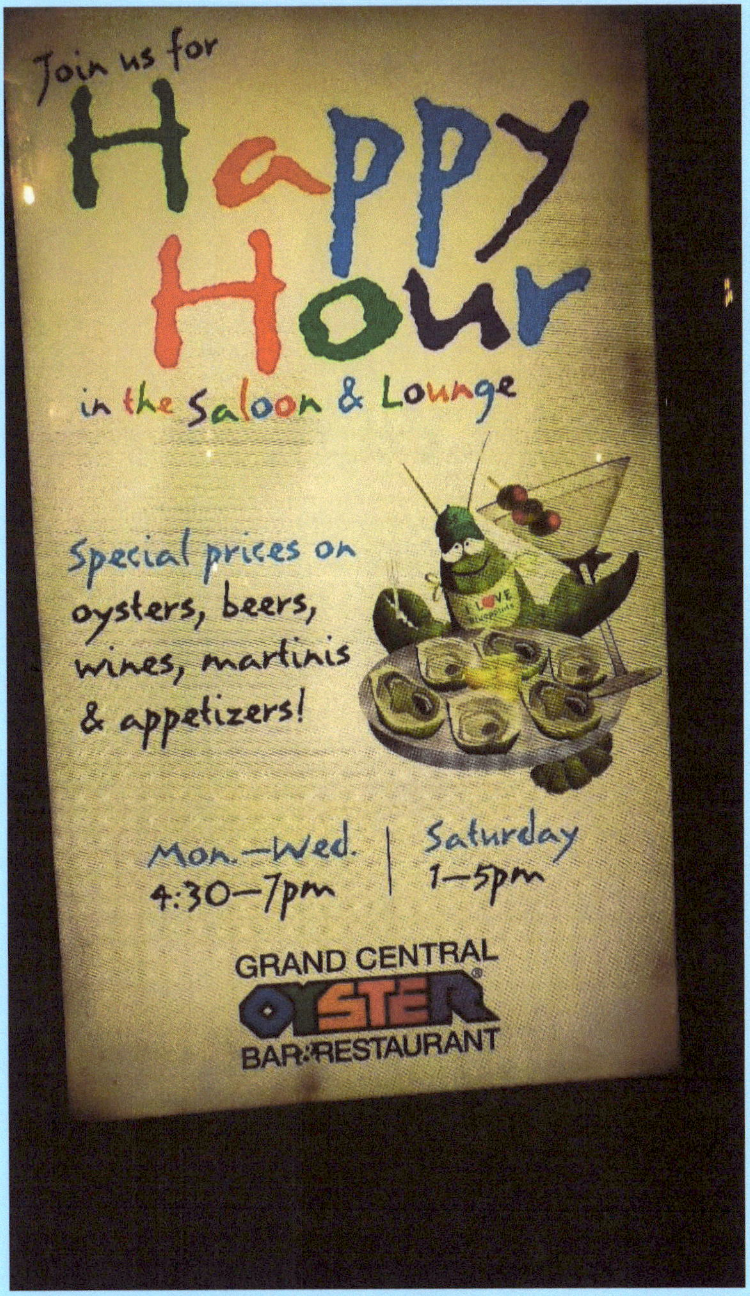

Join us for

Happy Hour

in the Saloon & Lounge

Special prices on oysters, beers, wines, martinis & appetizers!

Mon.–Wed. 4:30–7pm | Saturday 1–5pm

GRAND CENTRAL
OYSTER
BAR:RESTAURANT

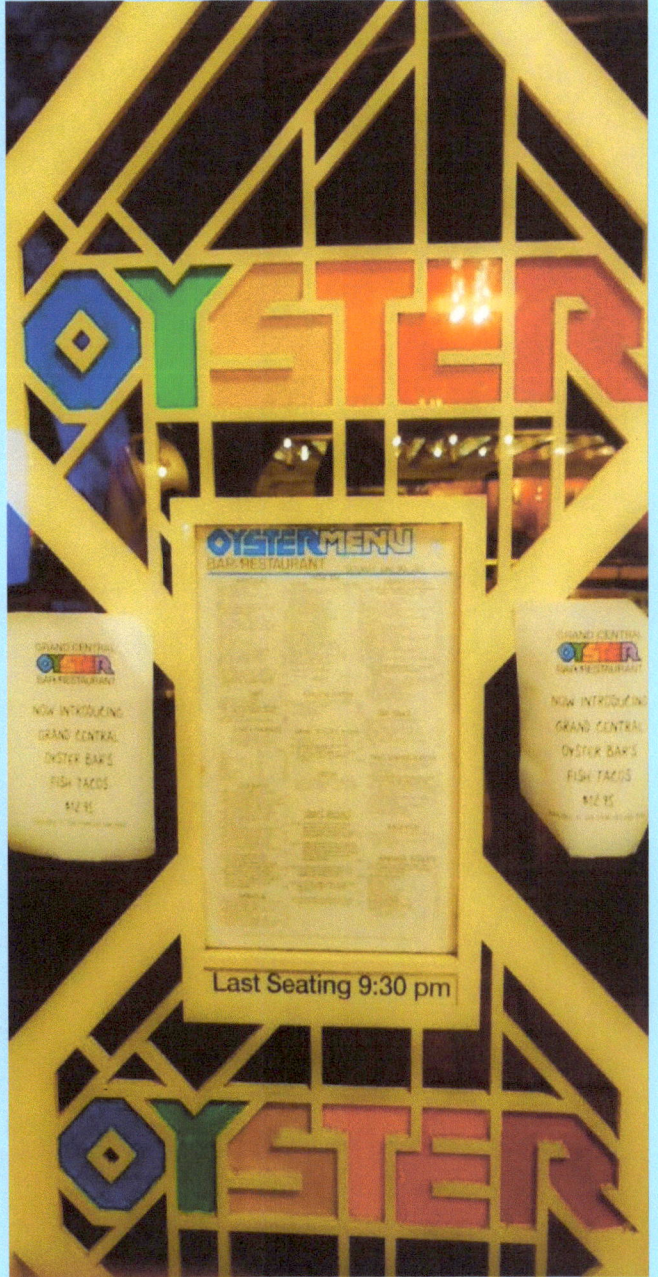

OYSTER

OYSTER MENU
BAR:RESTAURANT

Last Seating 9:30 pm

OYSTER

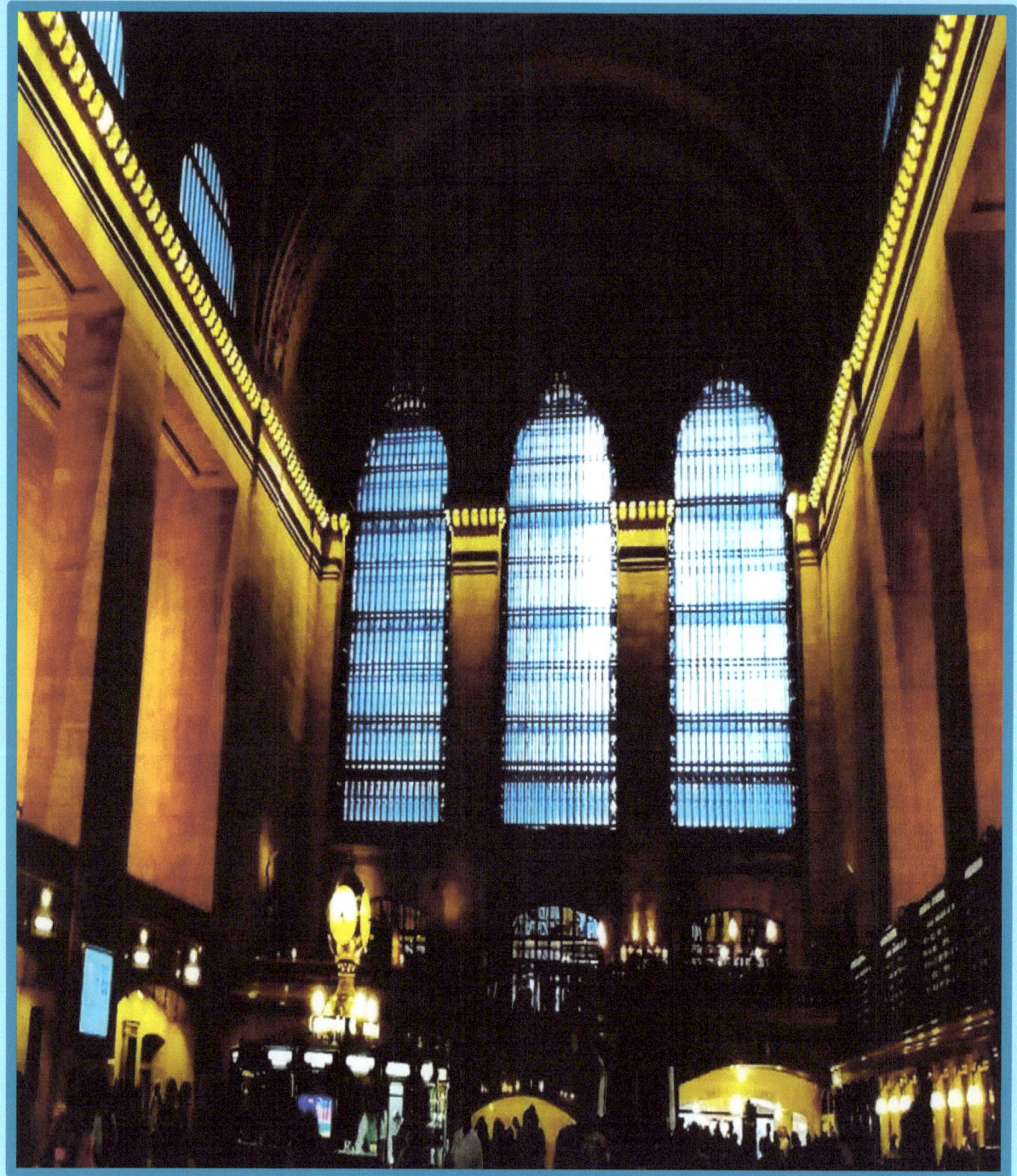

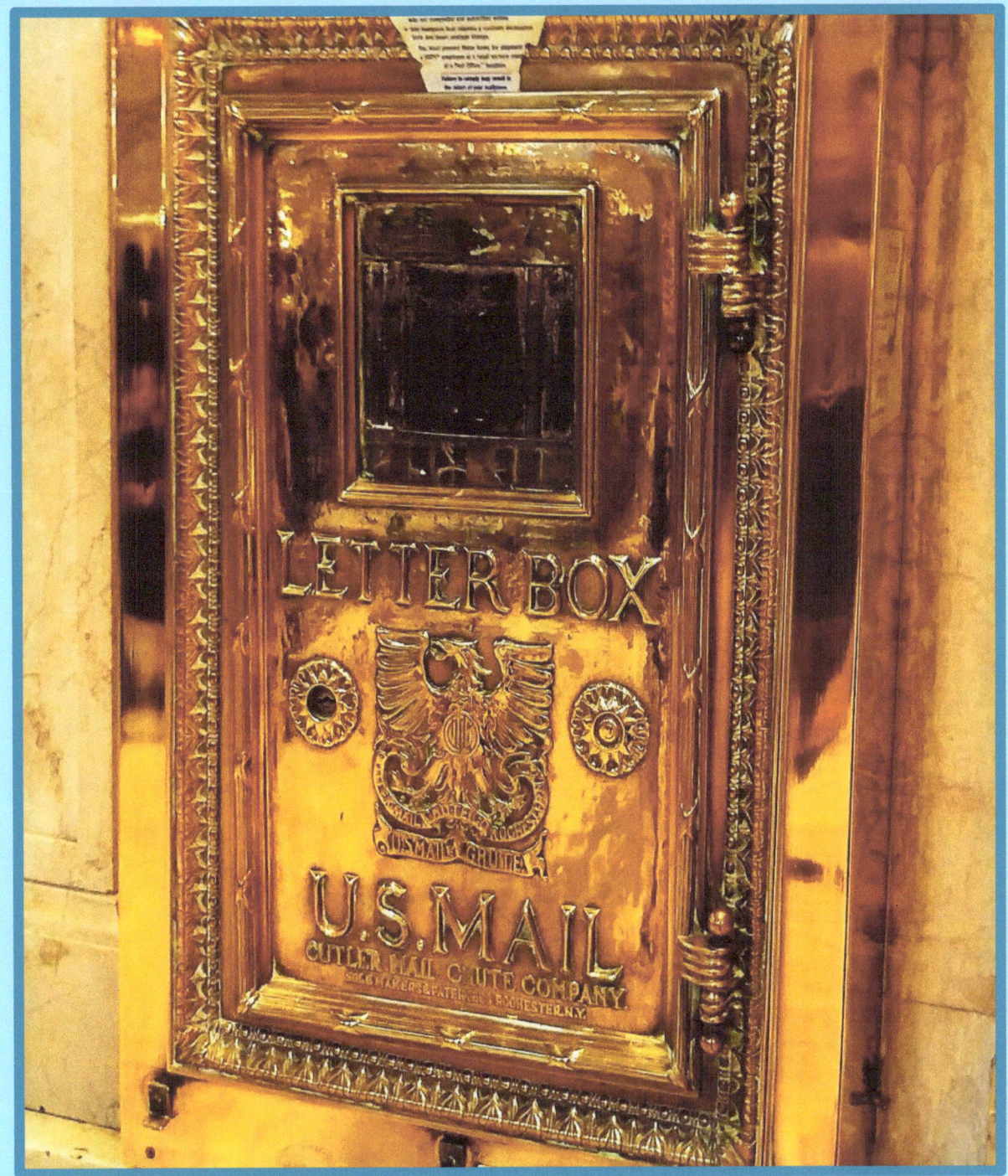

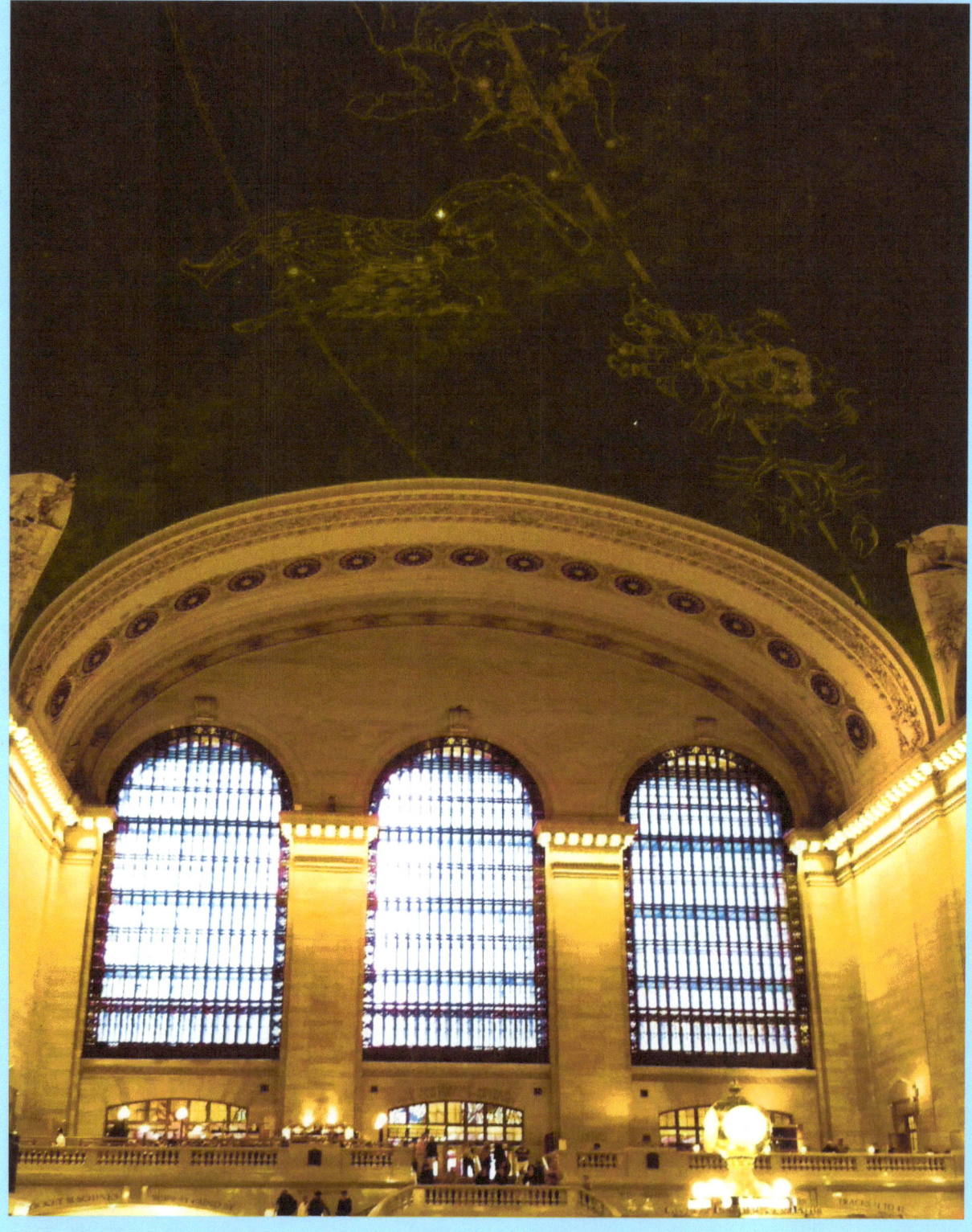

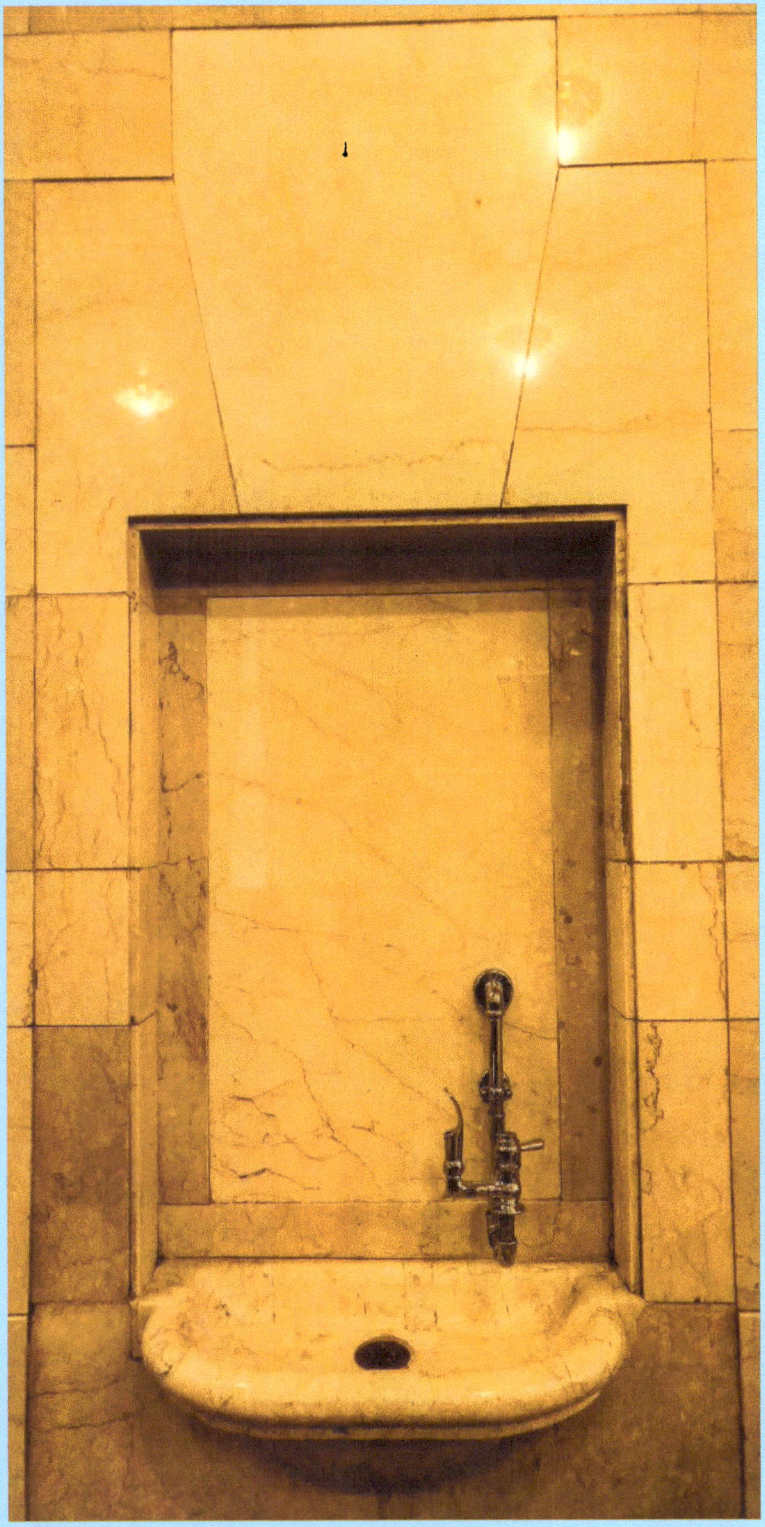

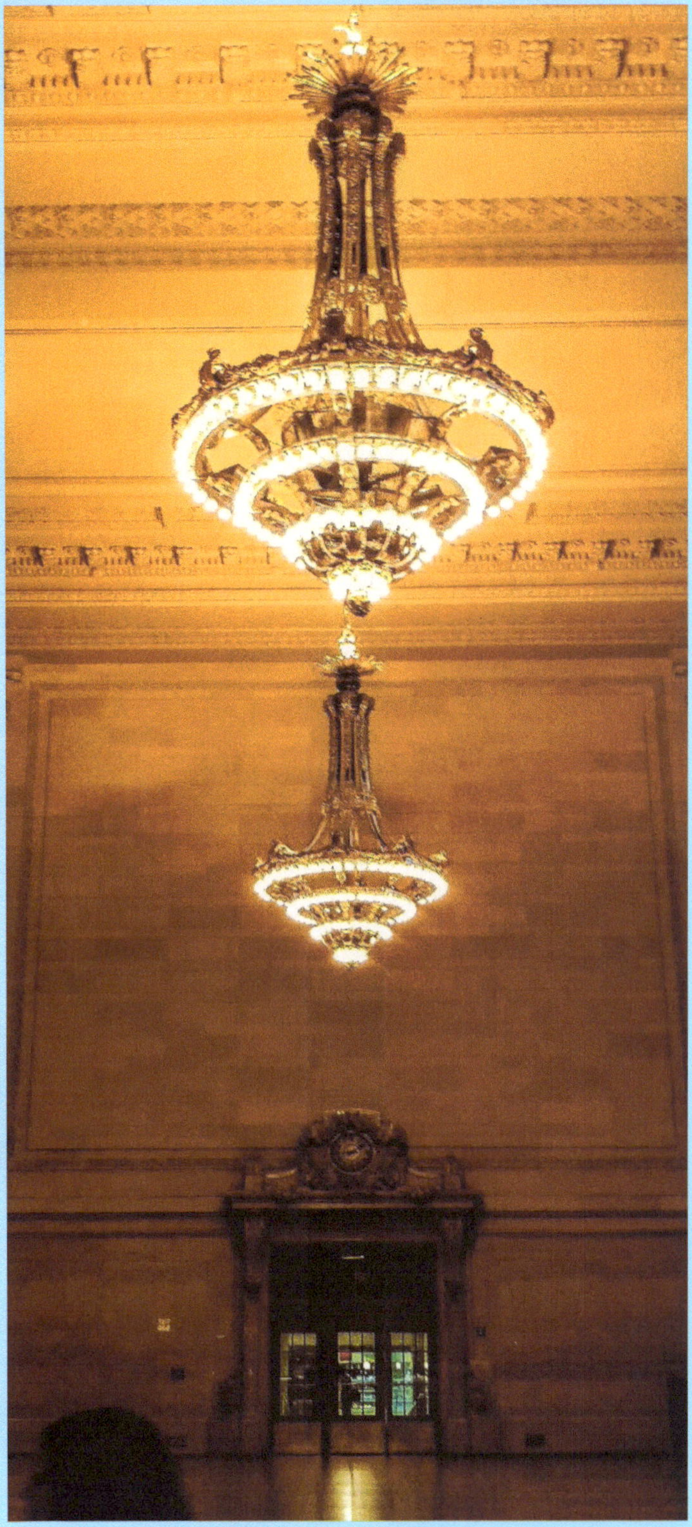

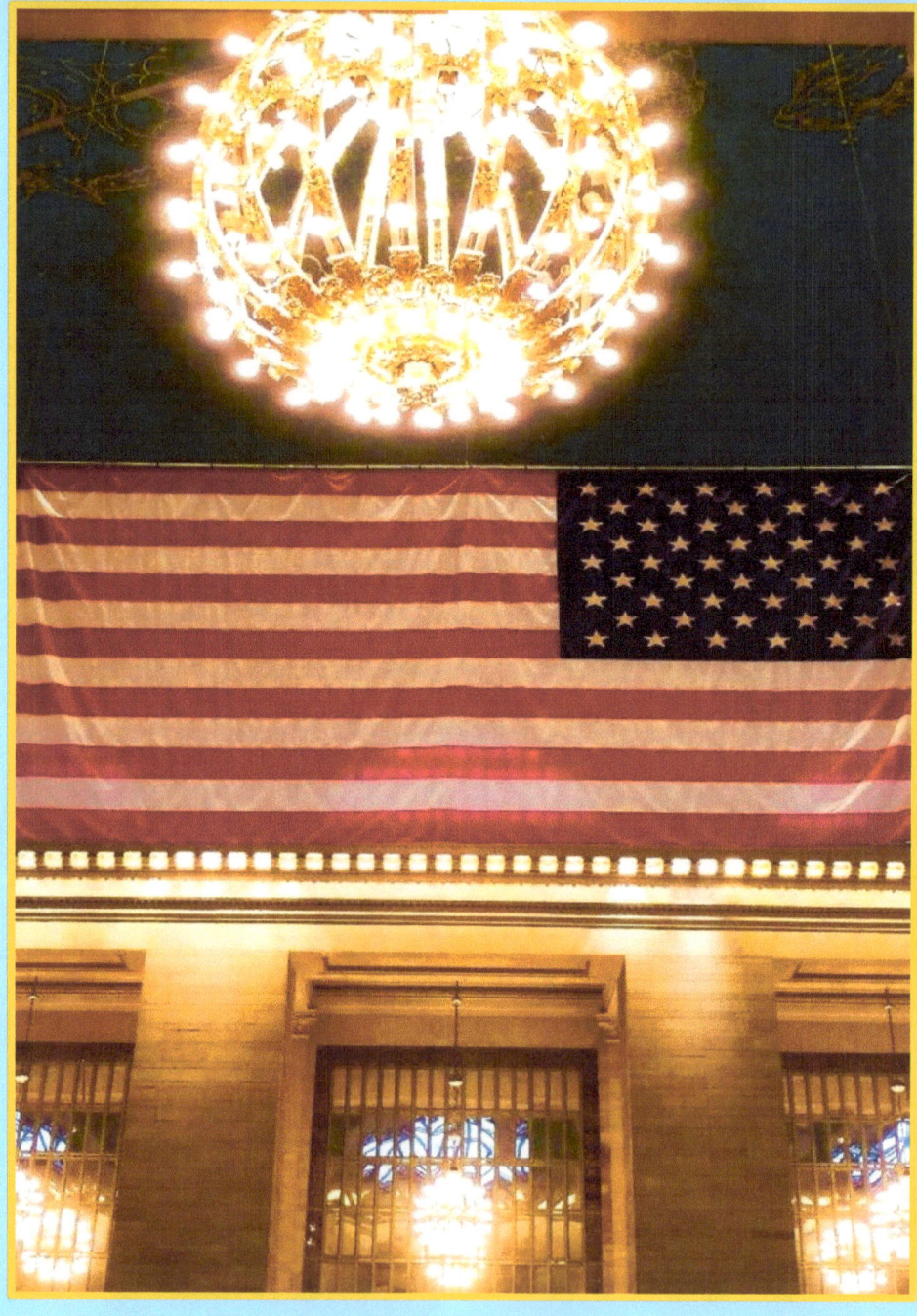

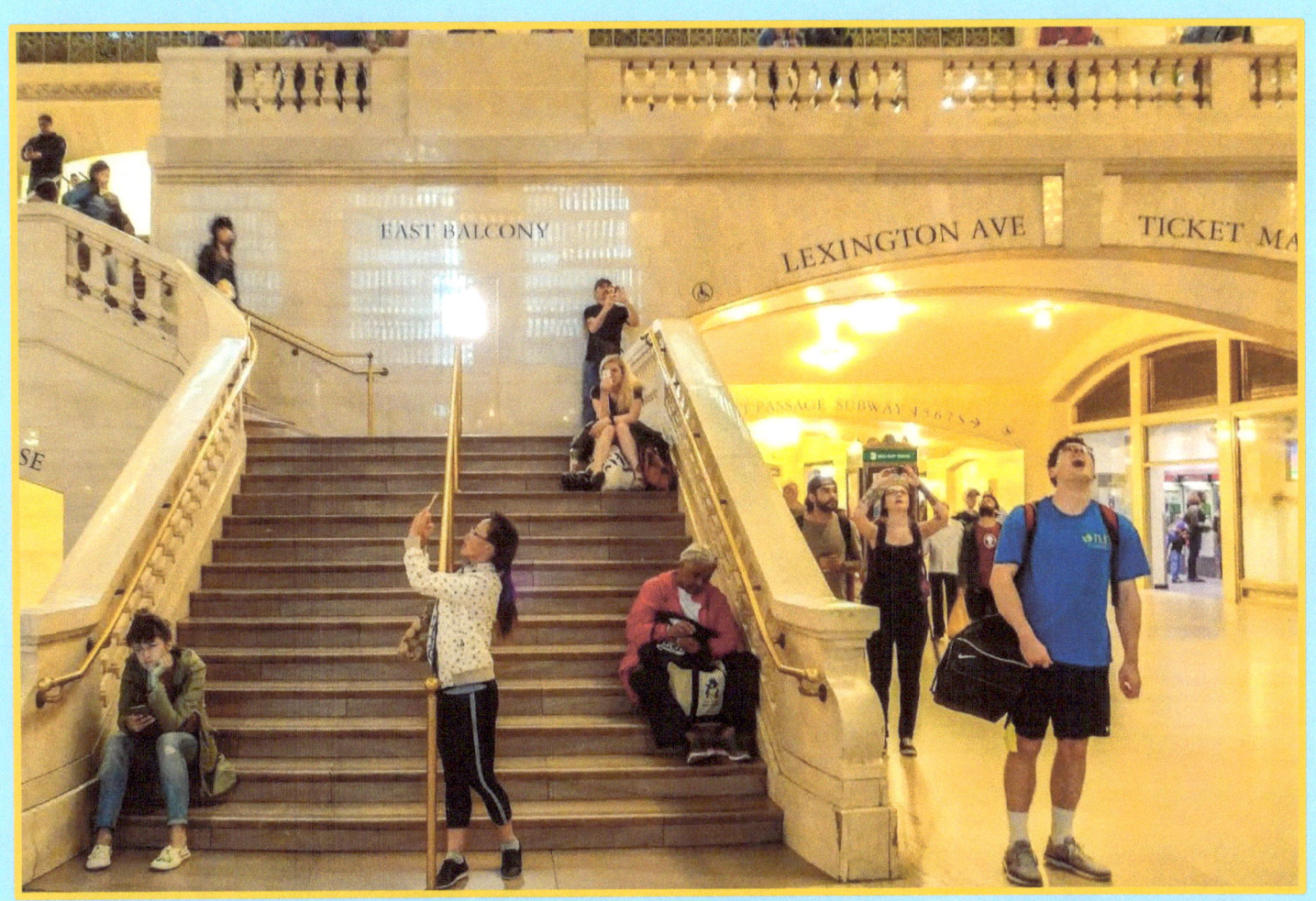

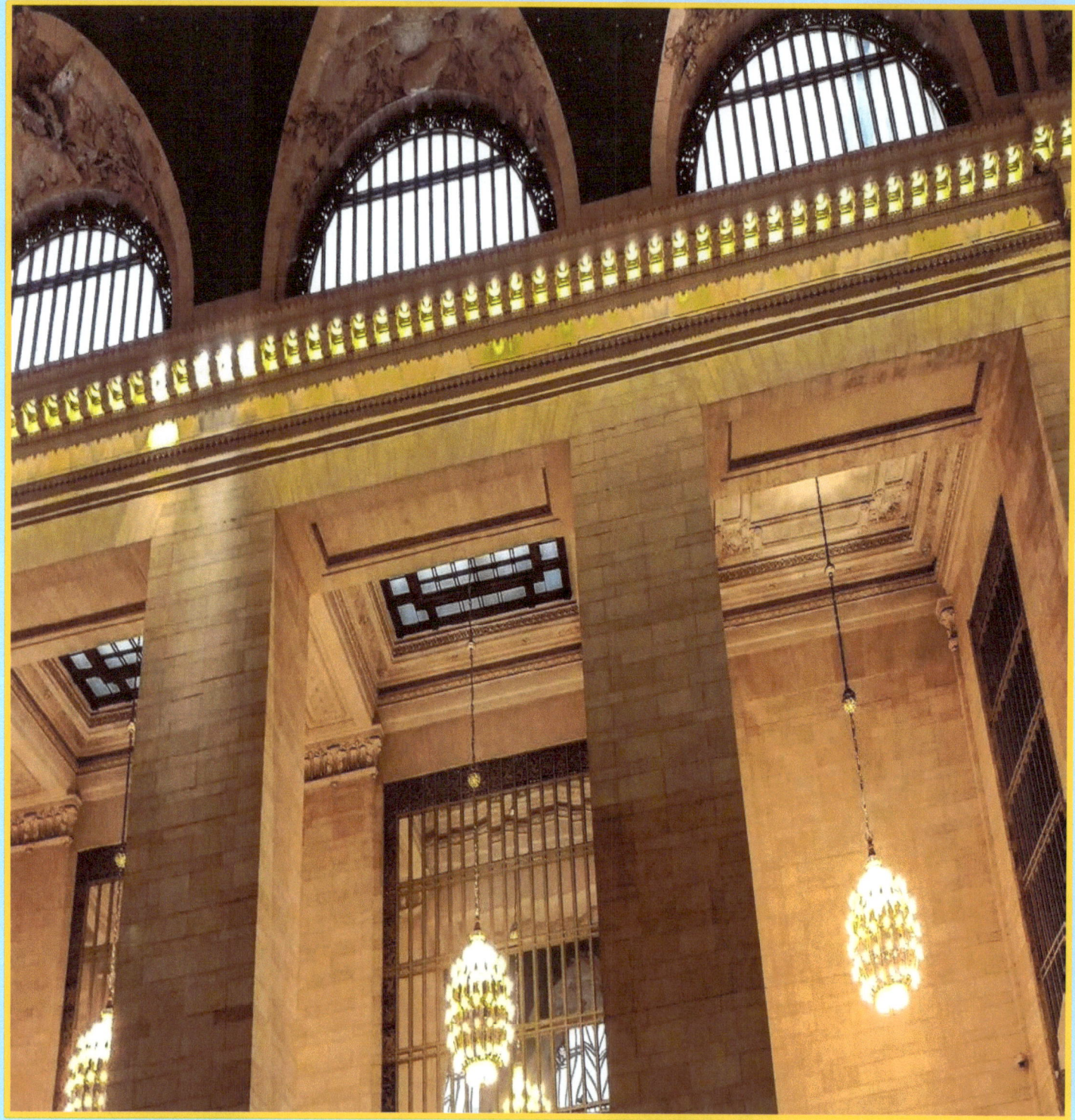

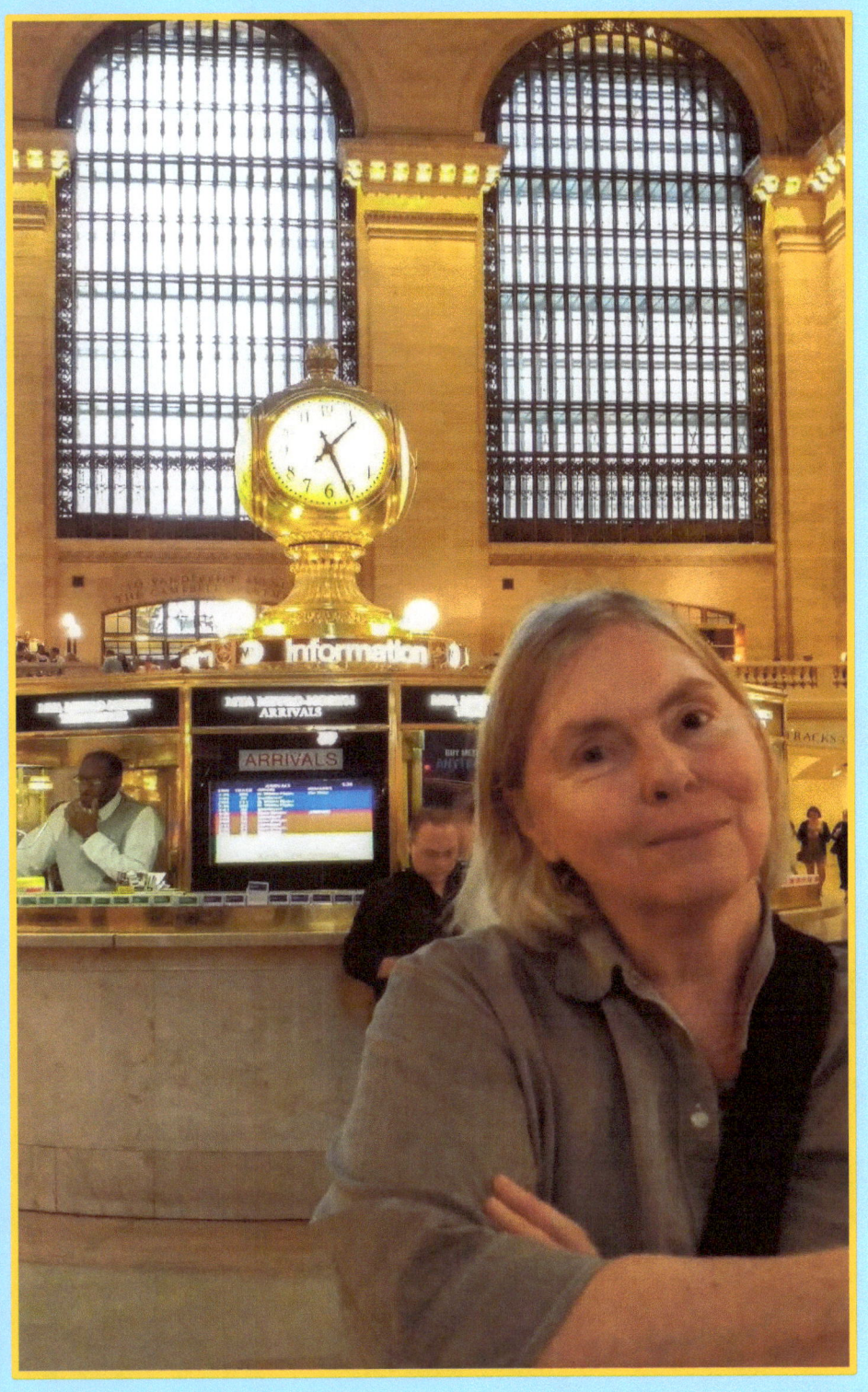

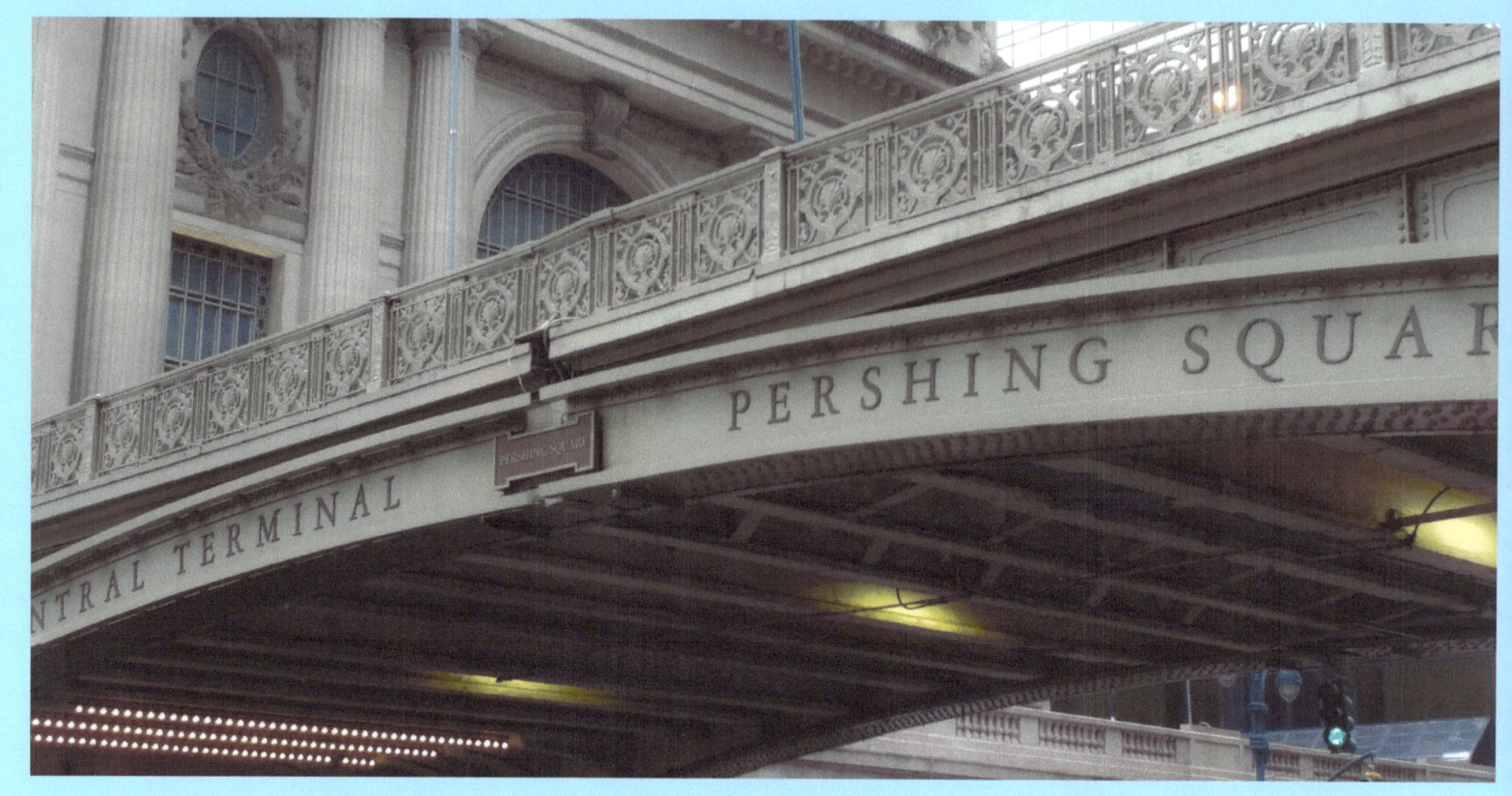

NEW YORK HAS A *GRAND* CENTRAL TERMINAL

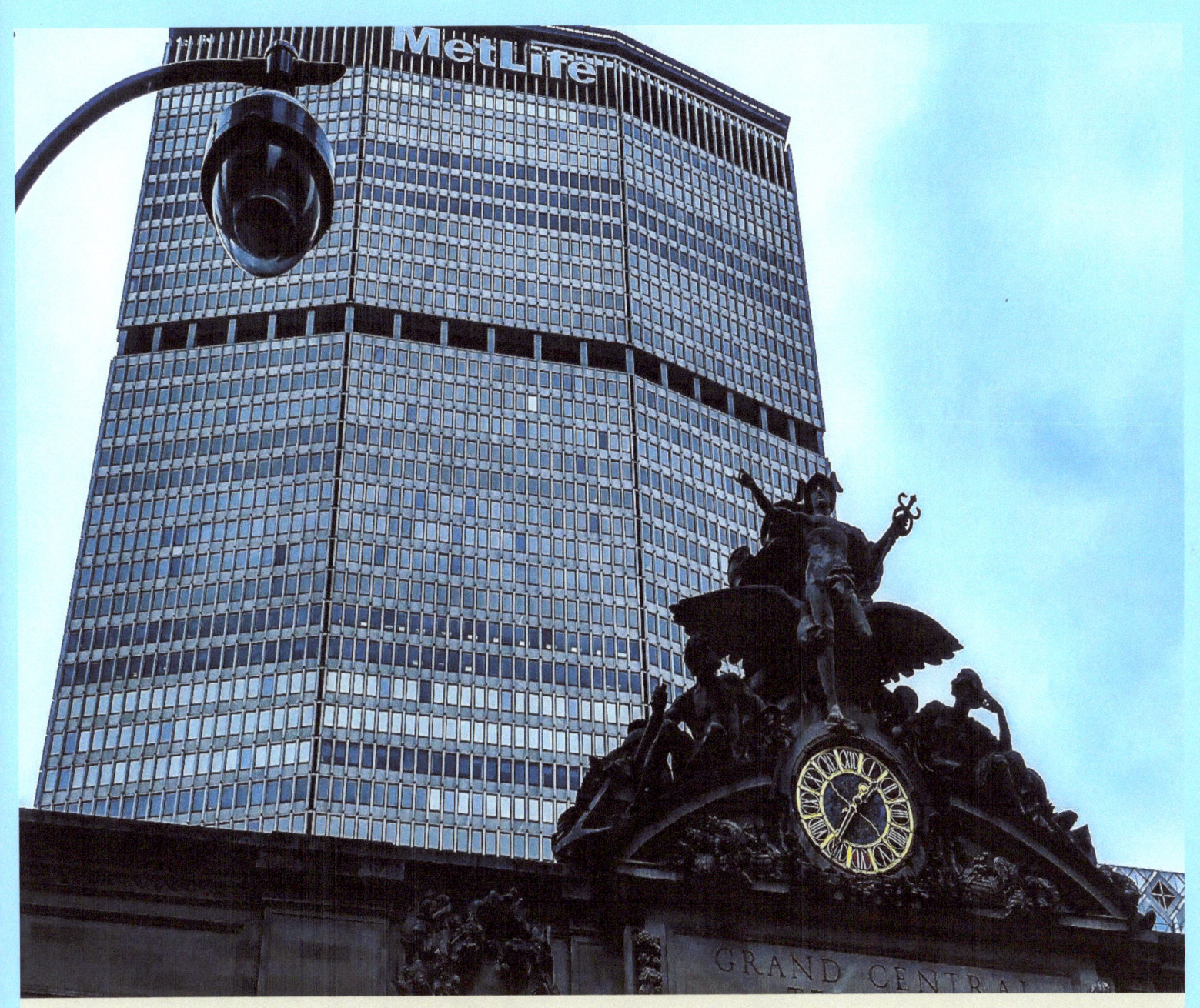

AND MANY OUTSTANDING
LANDMARKS

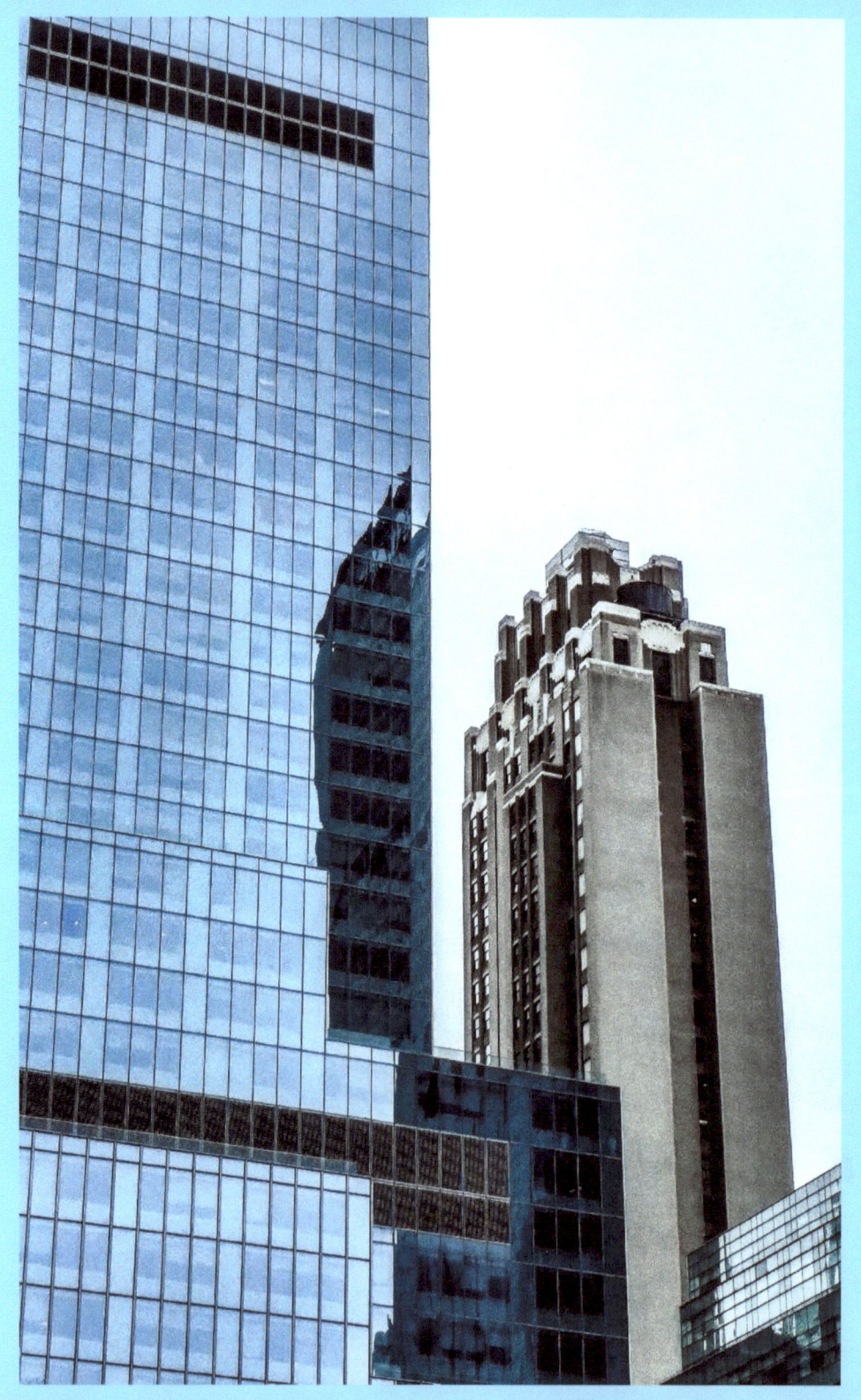

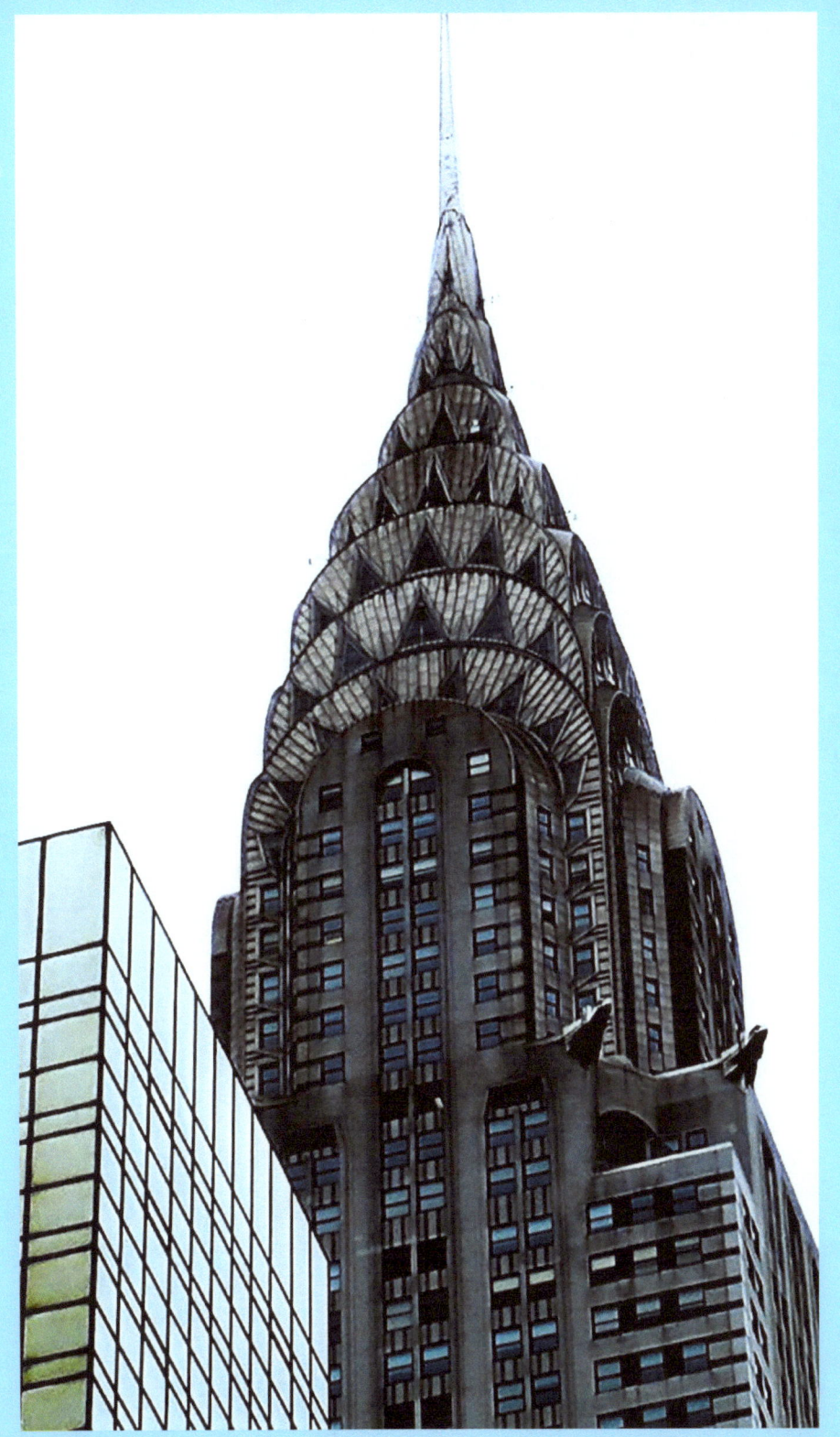

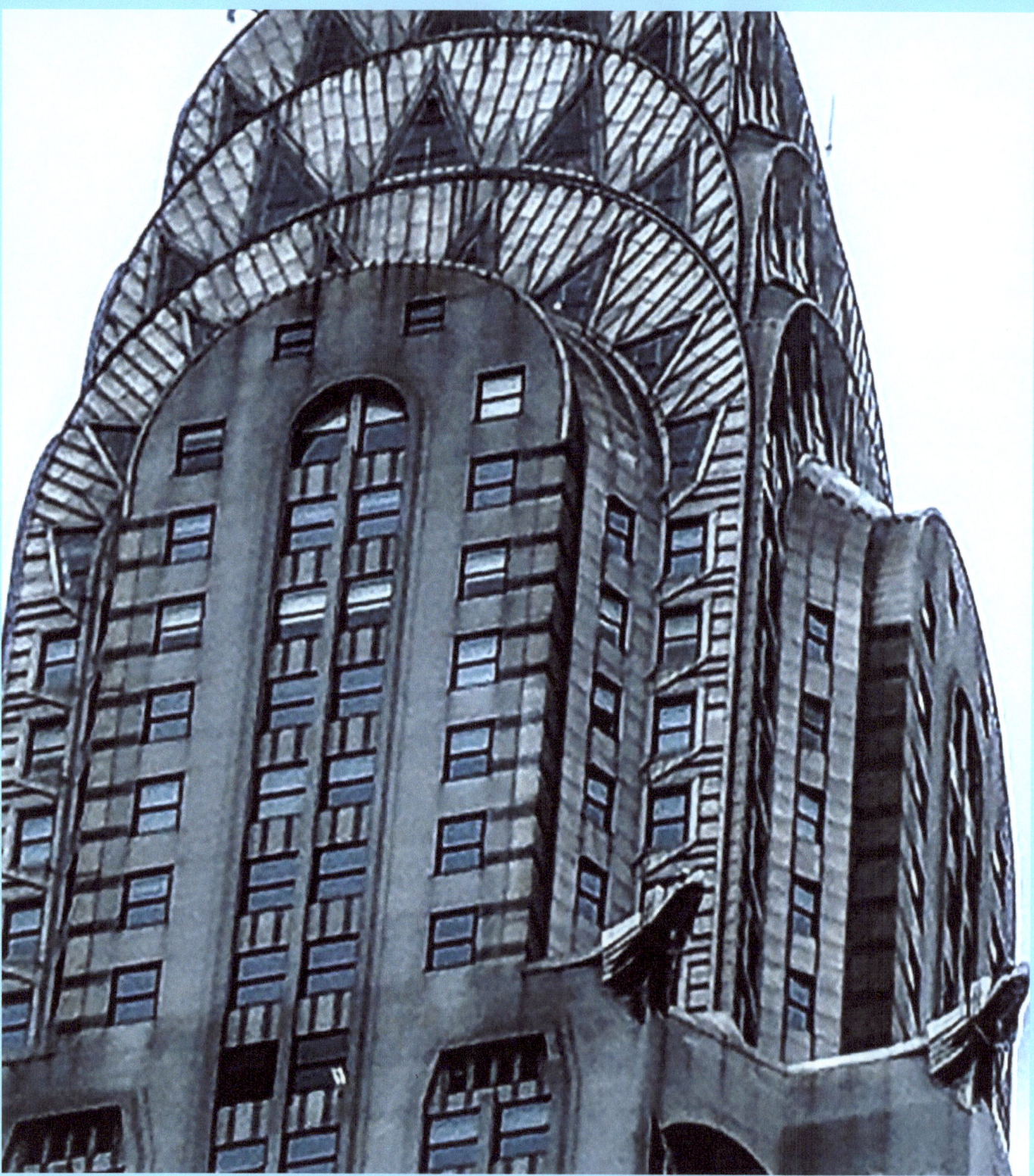

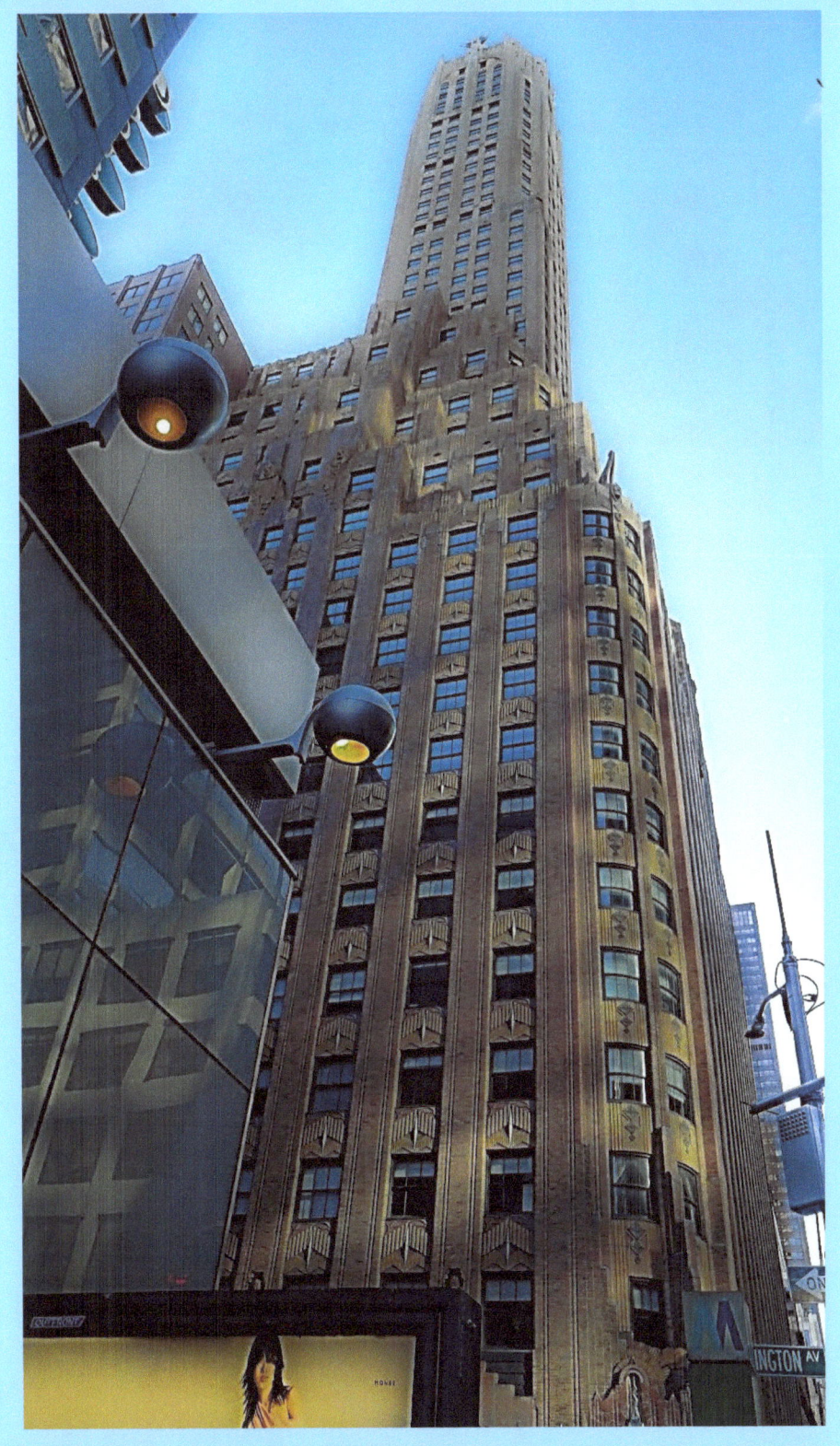

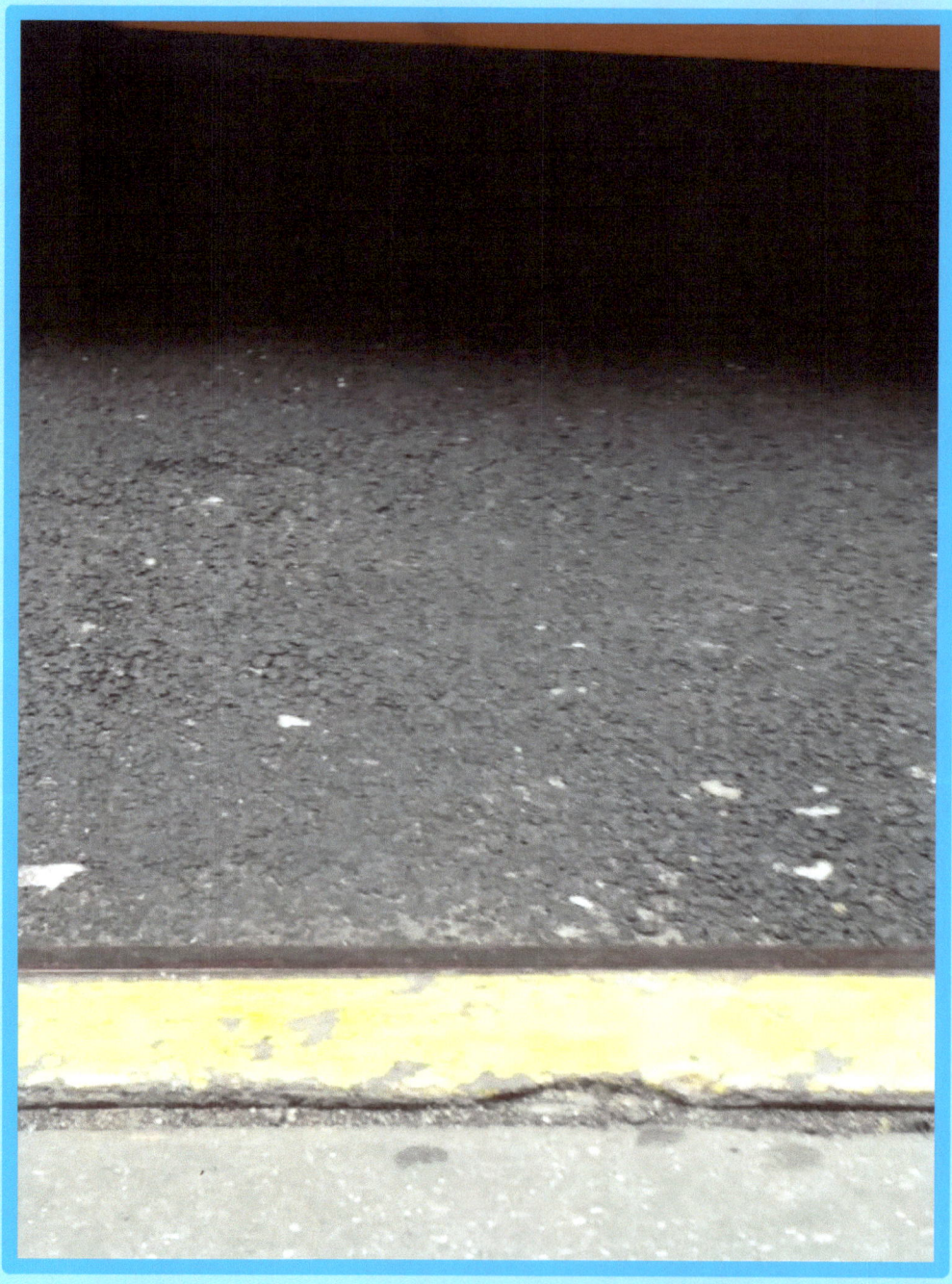

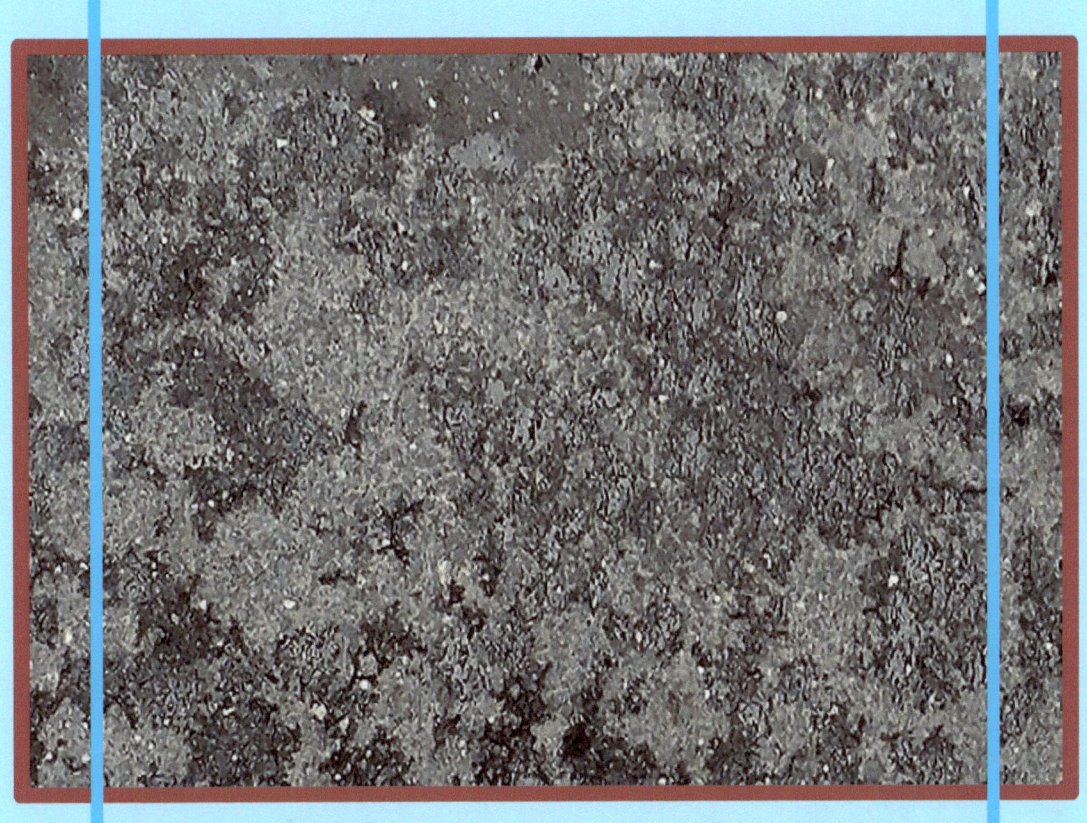

THE SIDEWALKS
OF NEW YORK

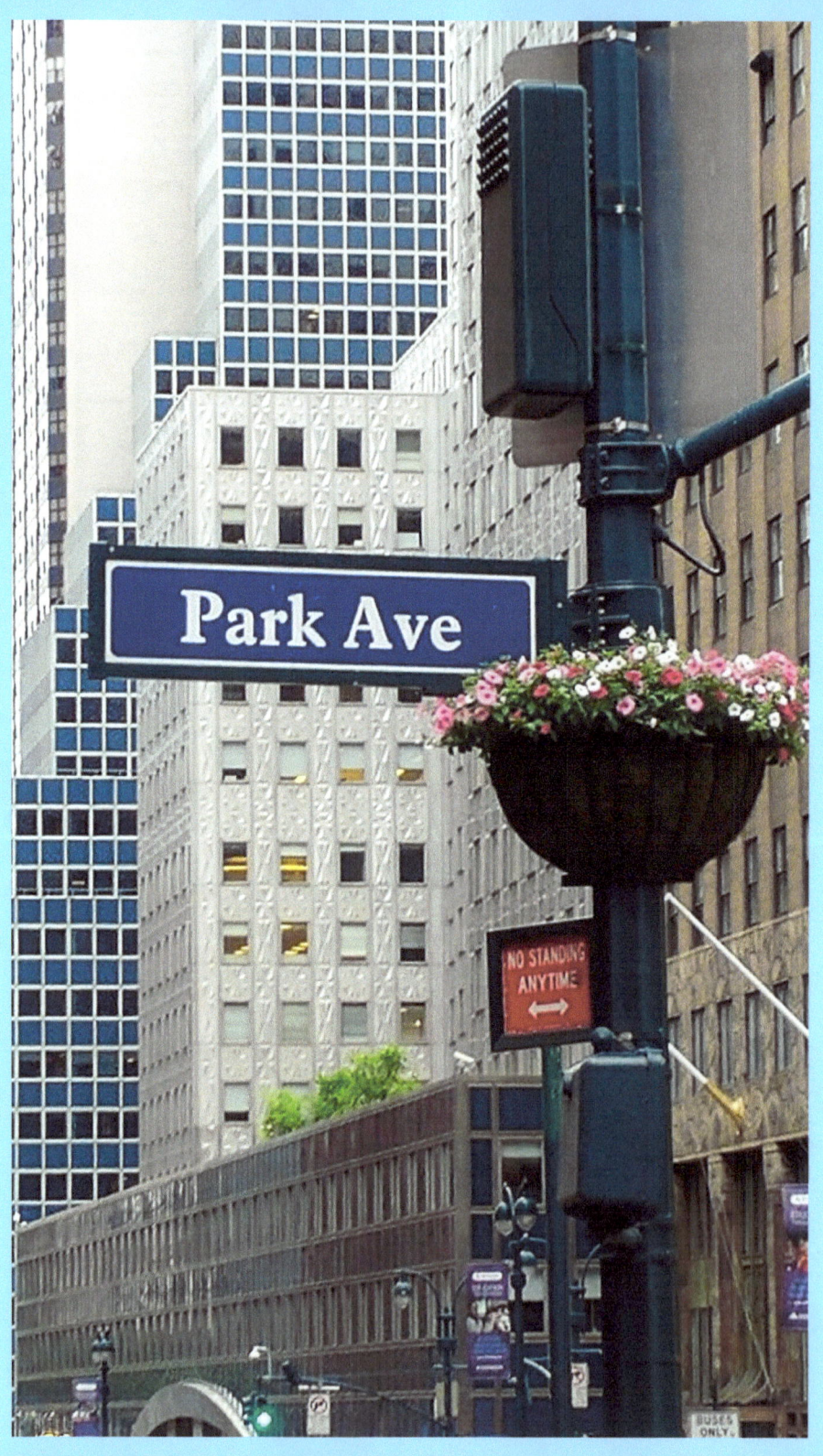

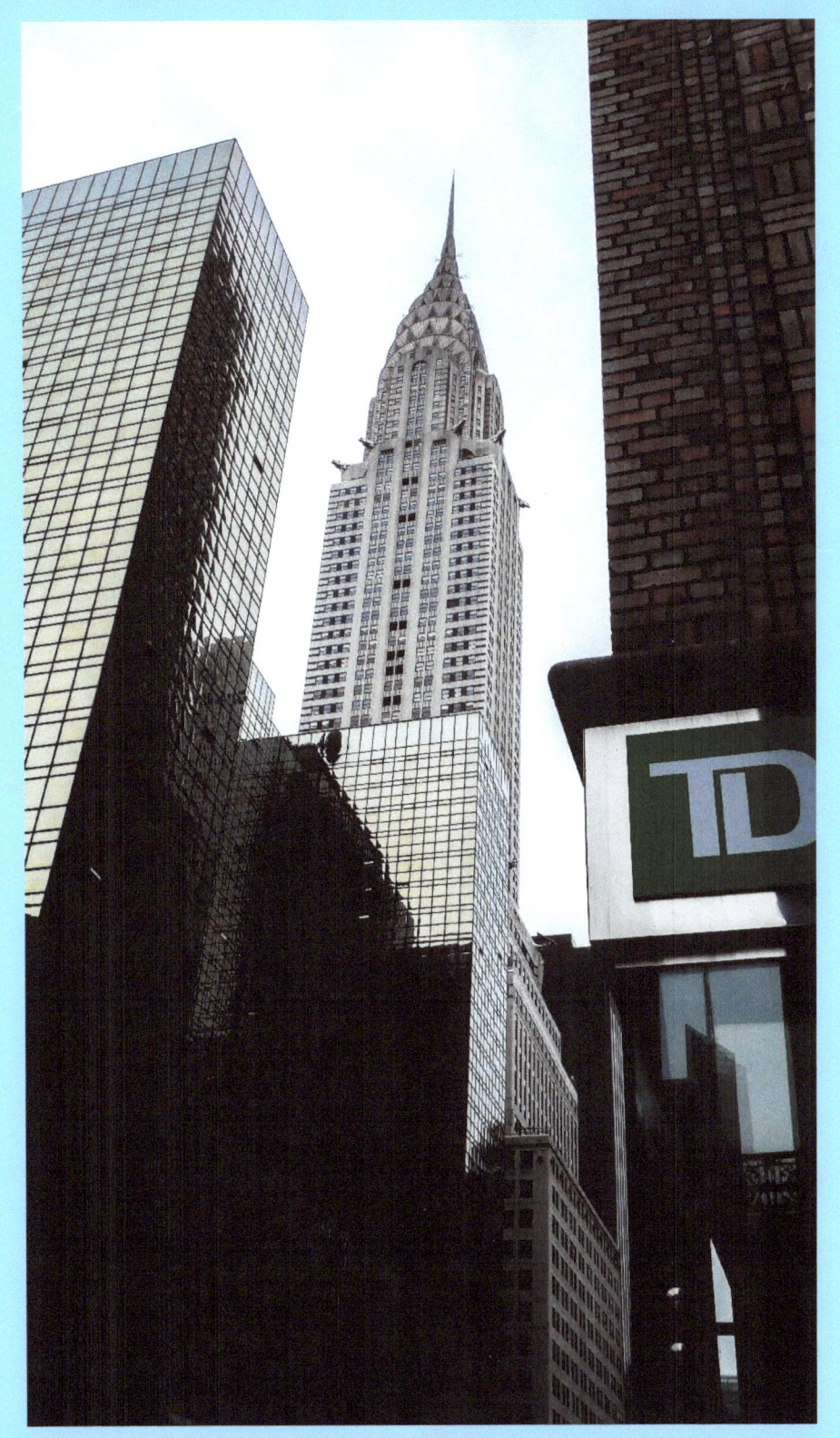

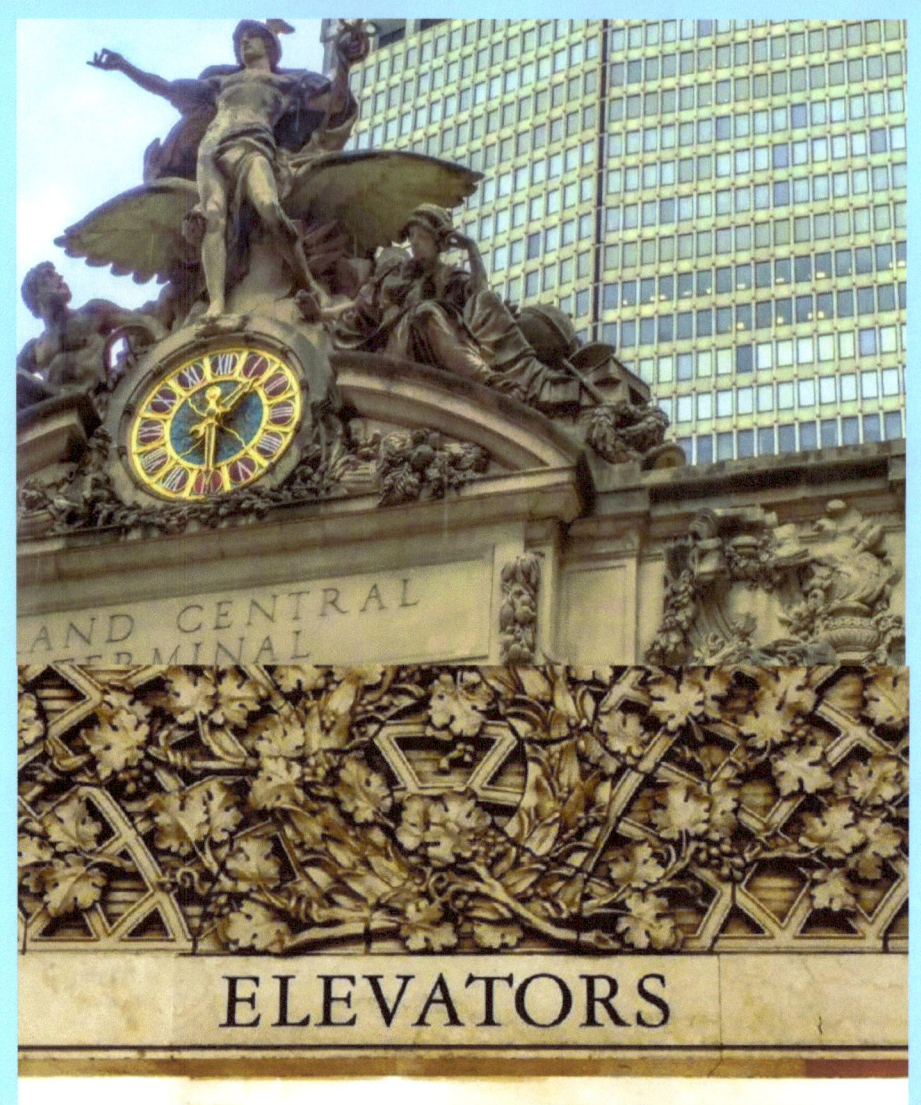

ELEVATORS

BENEATH THIS STATION
LIES A FRESH FOODS WONDERLAND,
WHERE THE SUMPTUOUS DISPLAYS ARE
NEARLY OVERWHELMING.

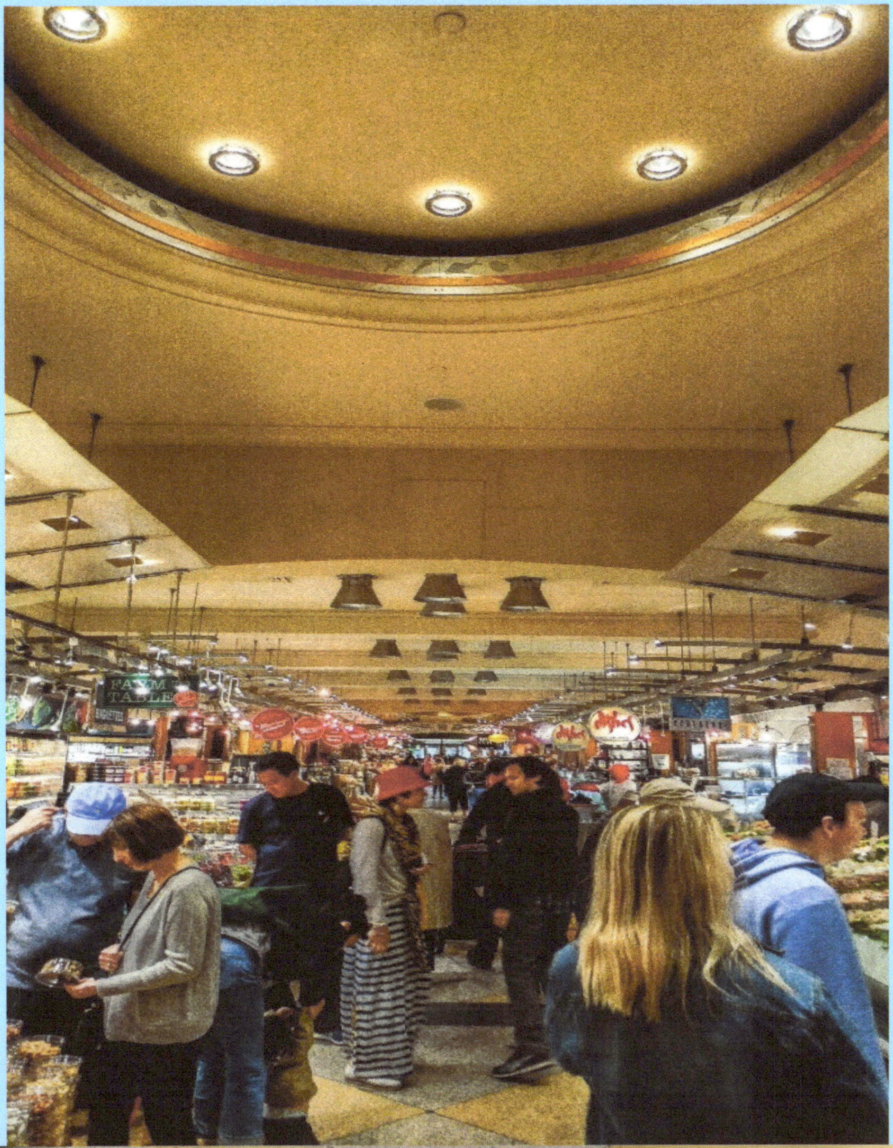

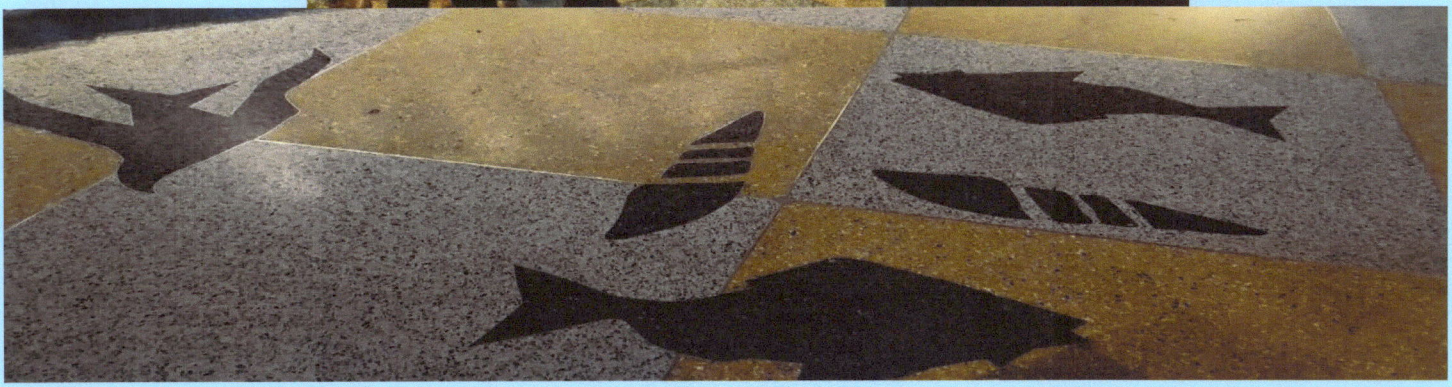

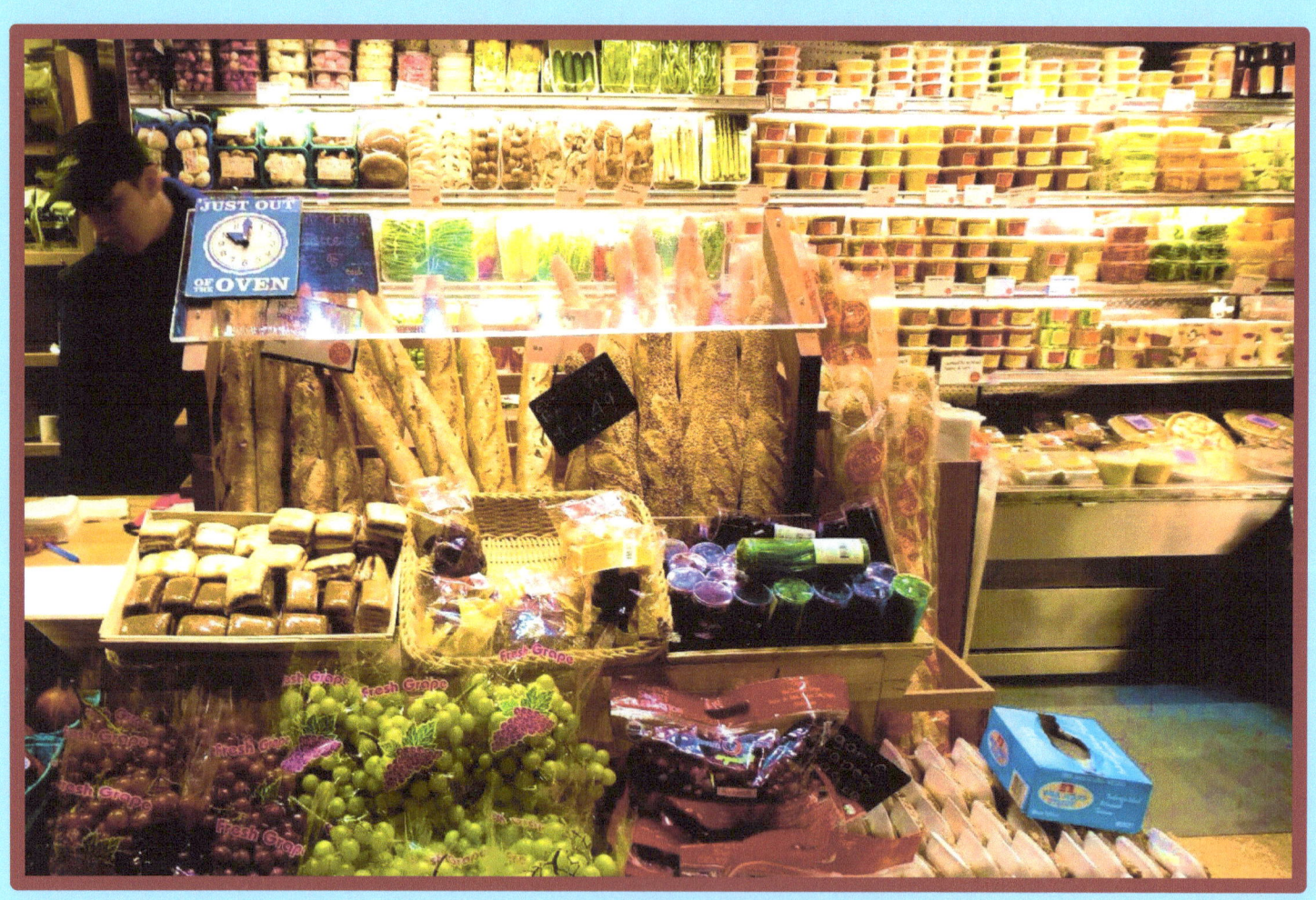

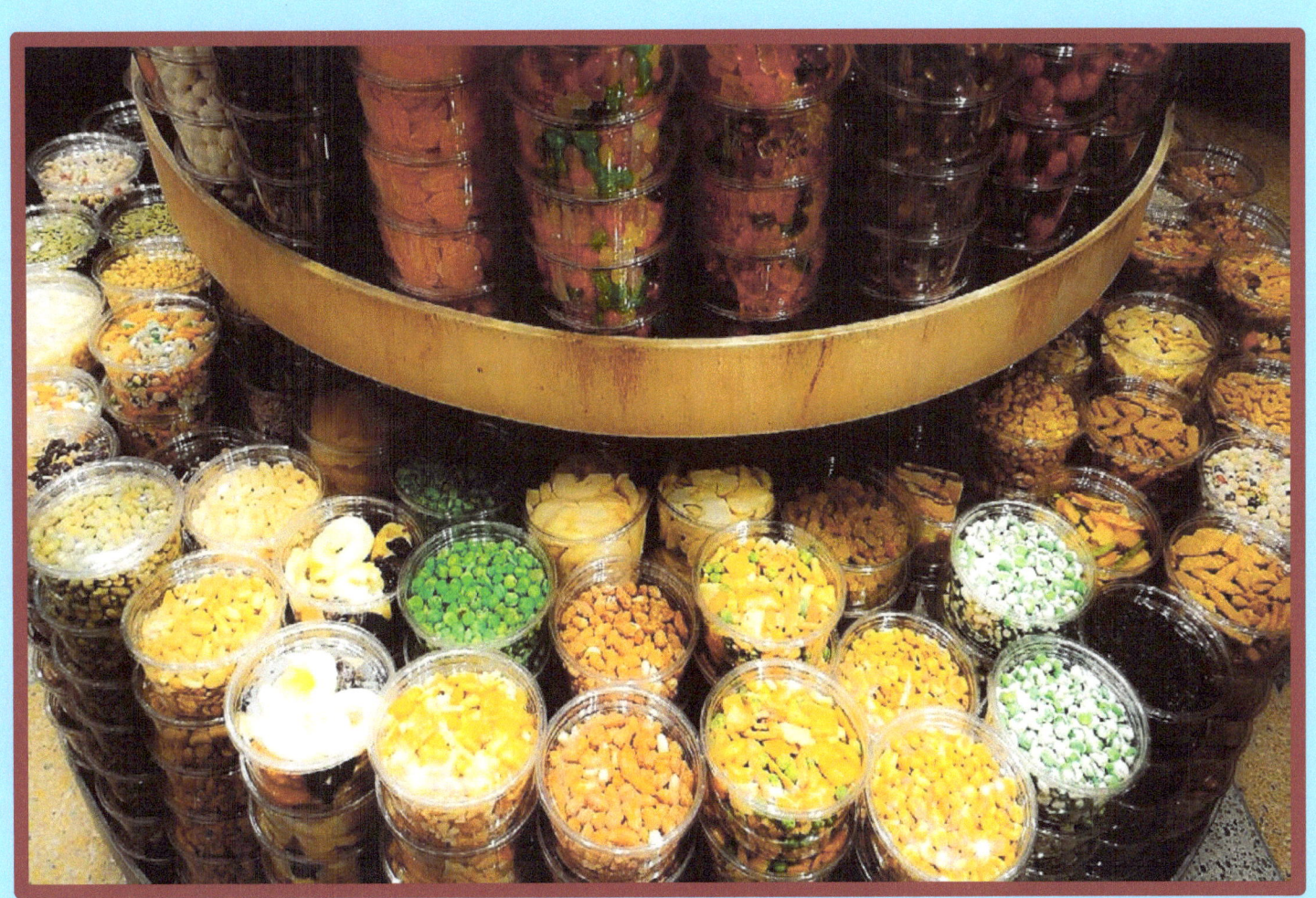

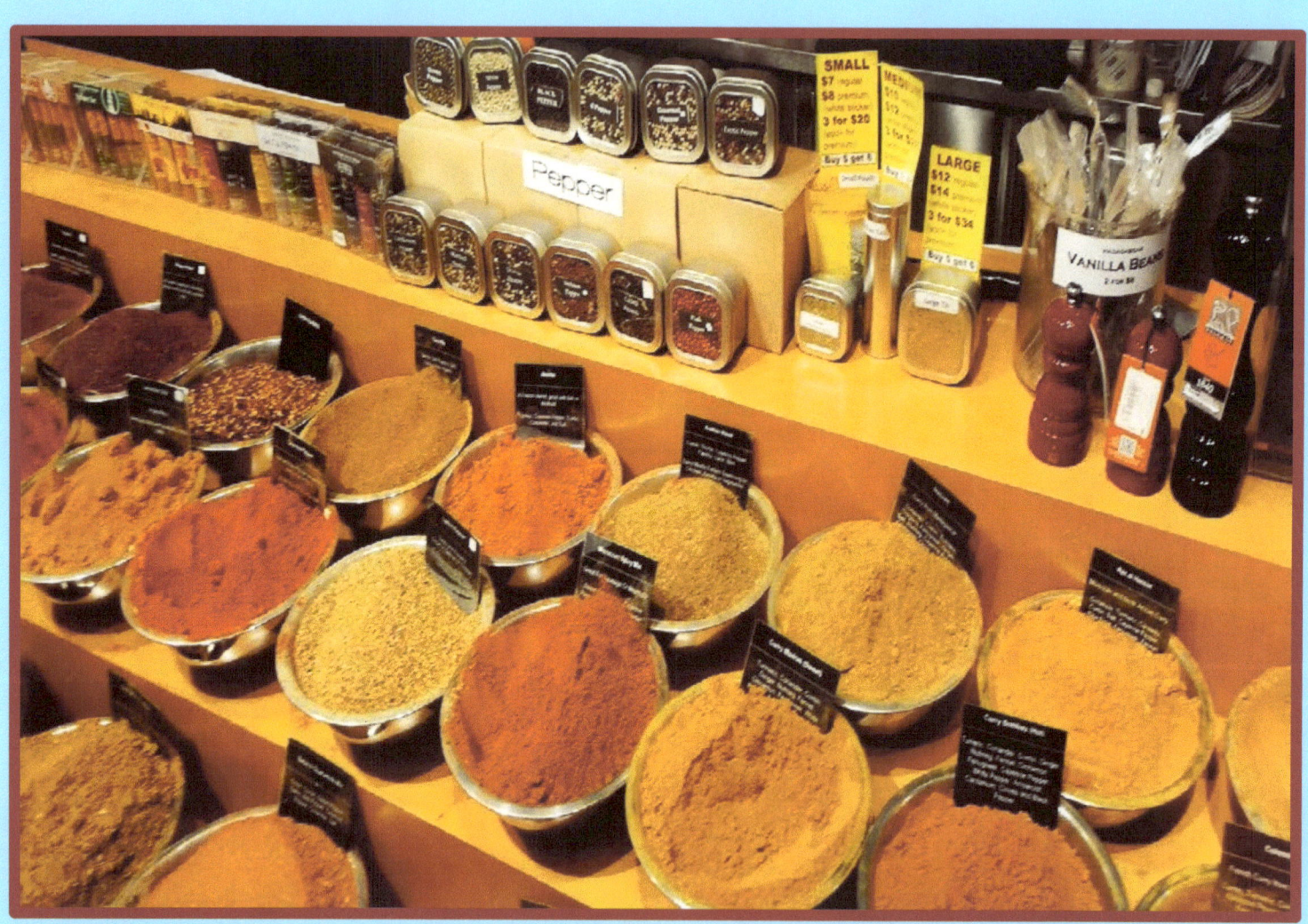

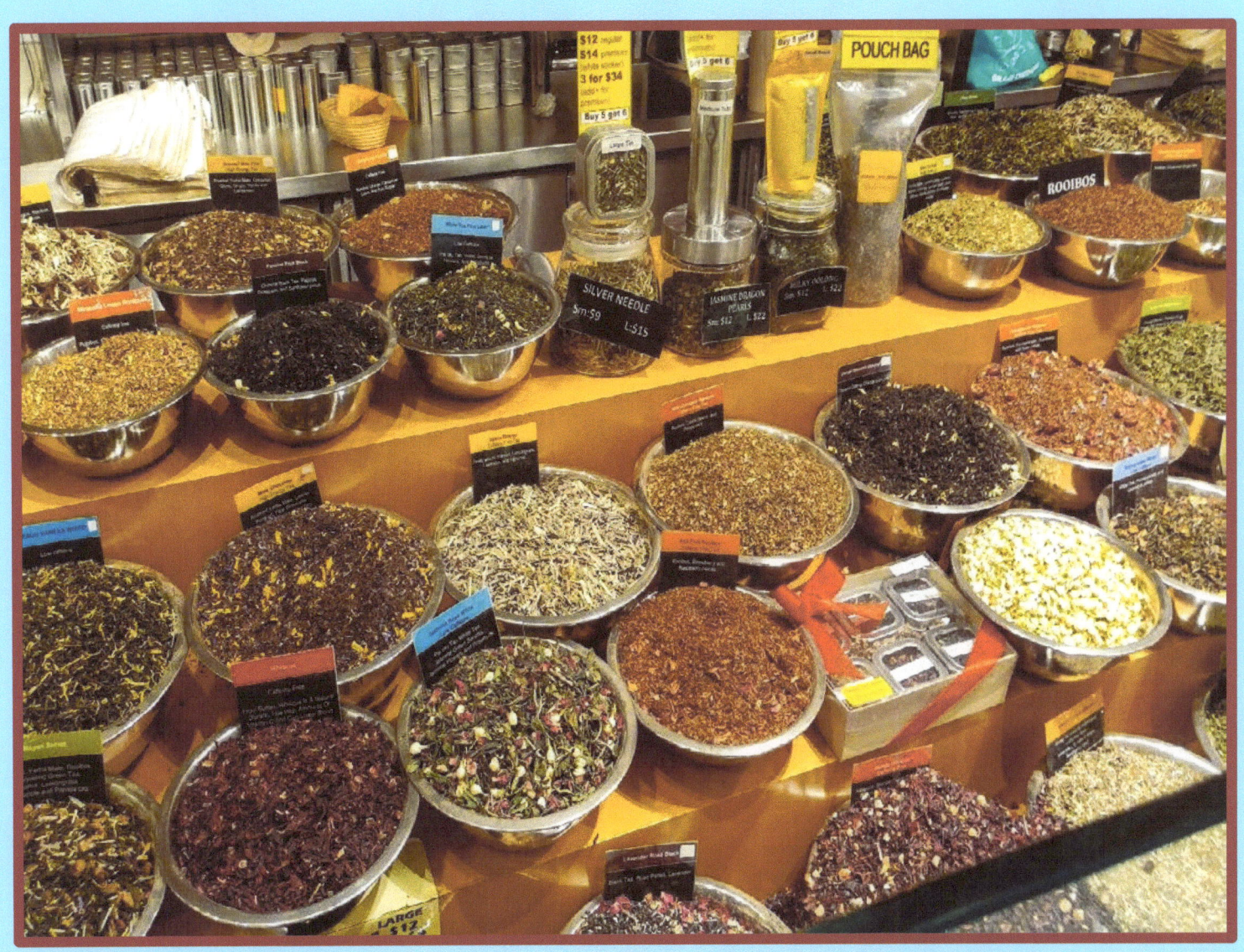

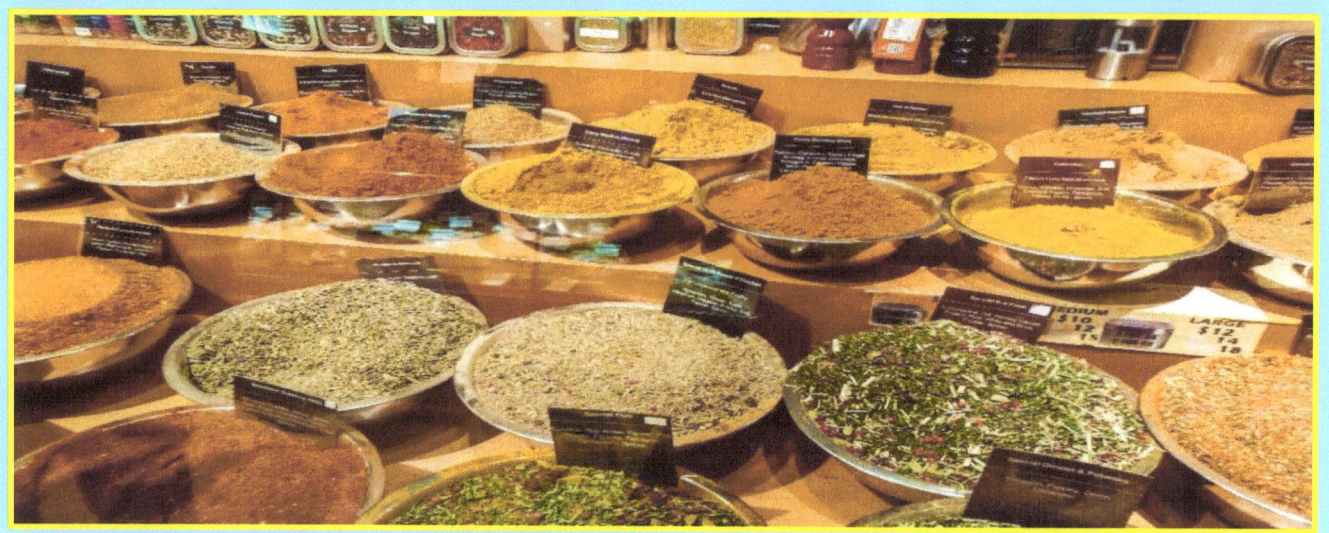

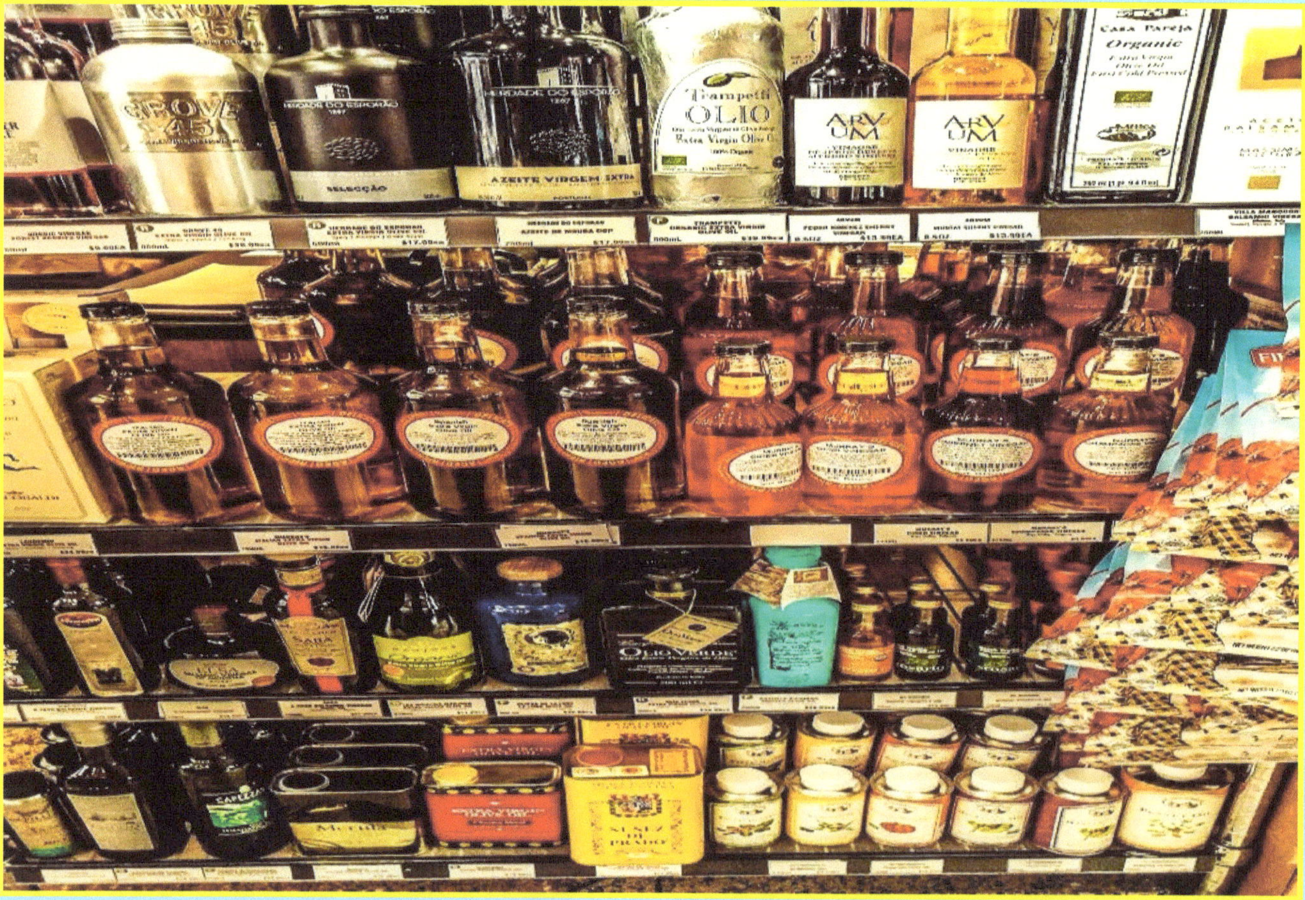

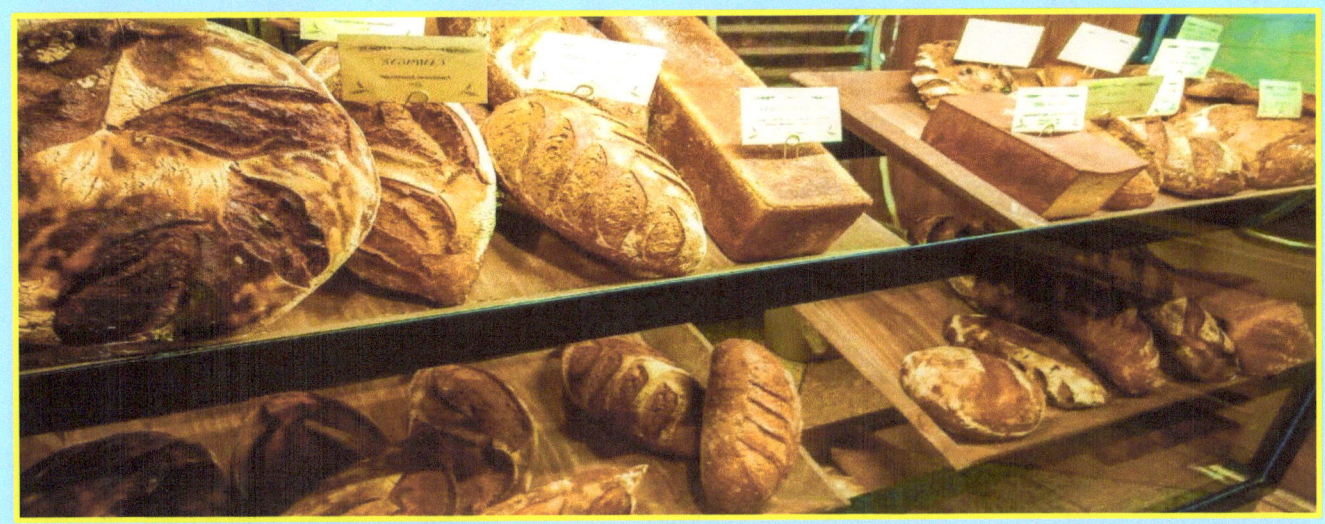

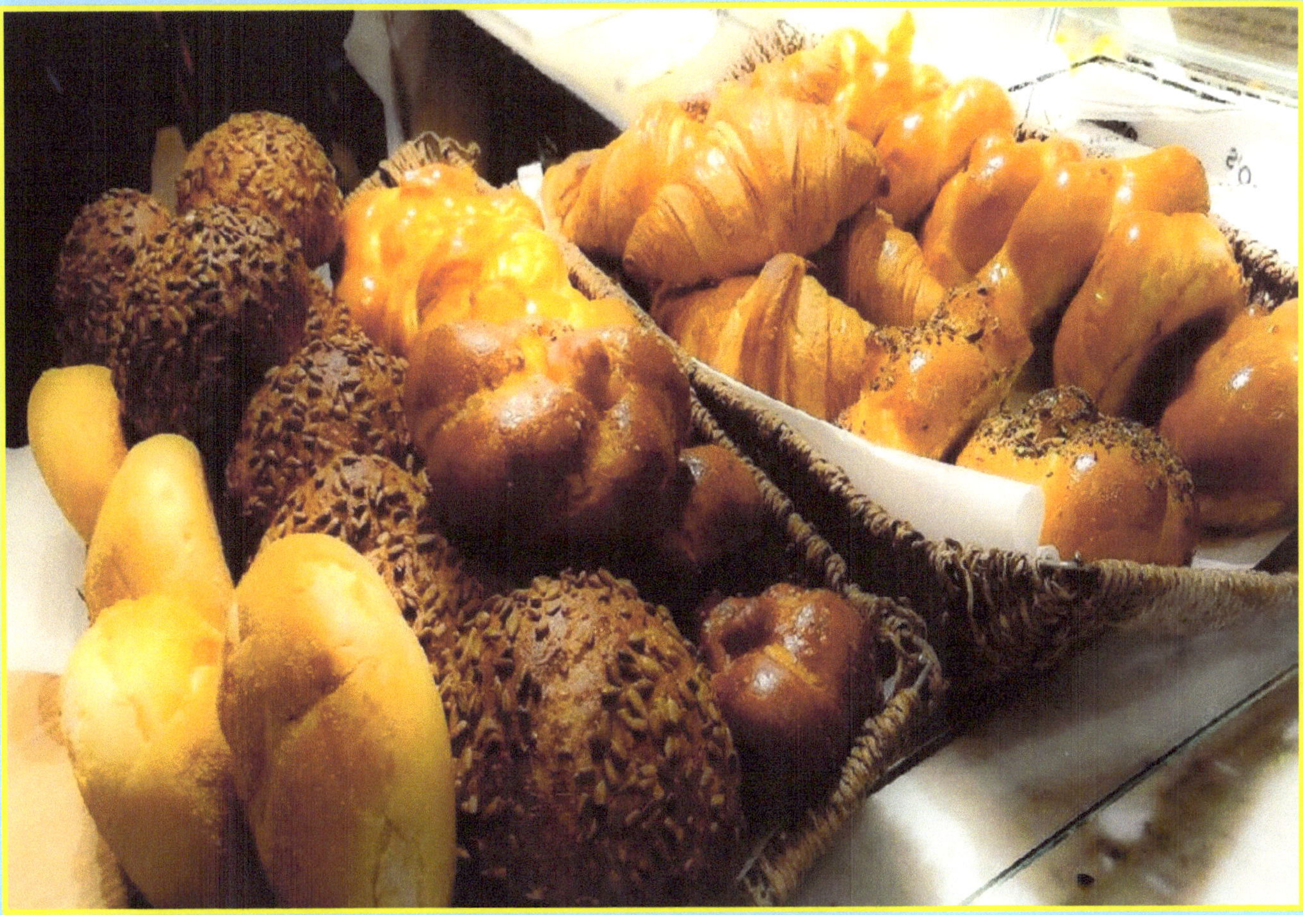

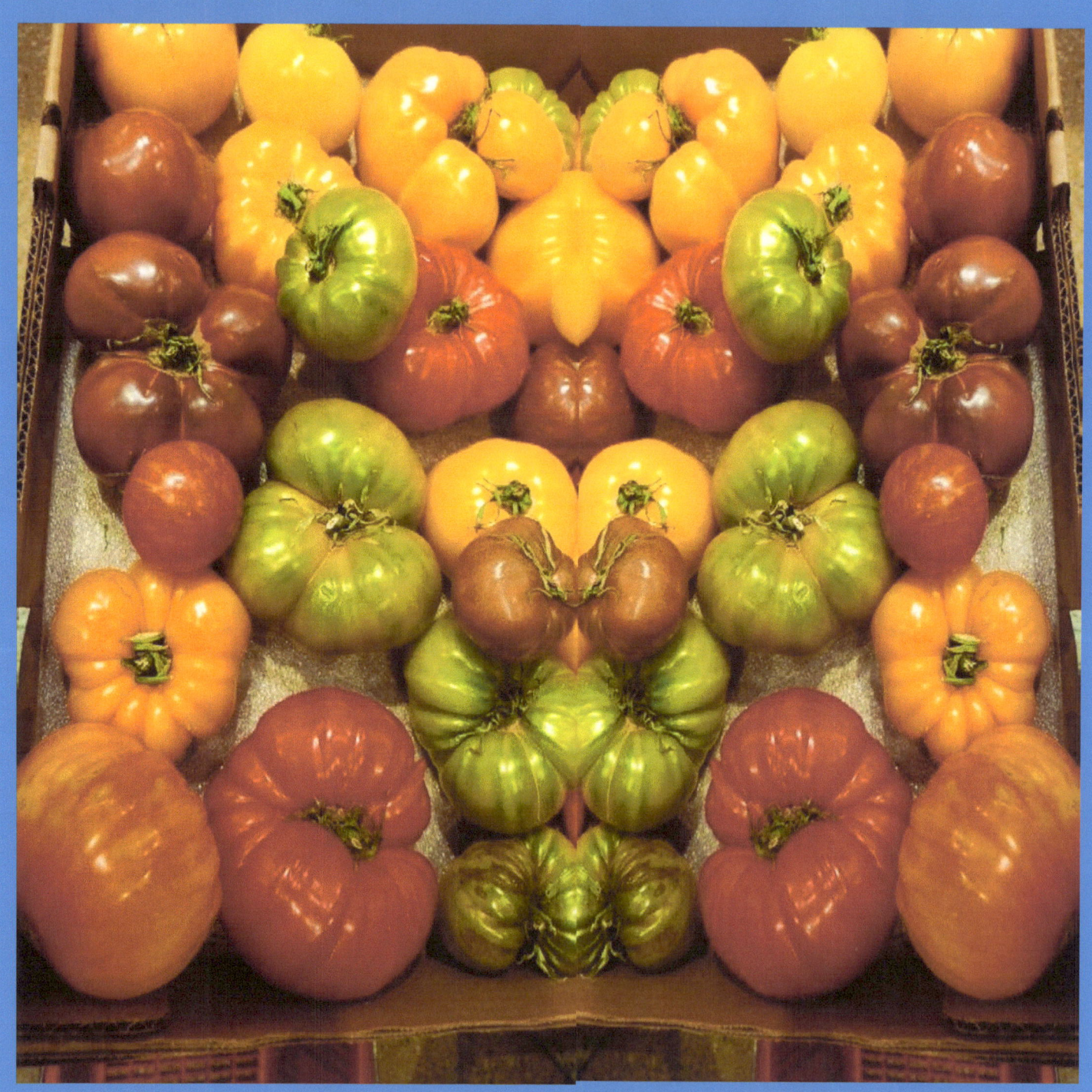

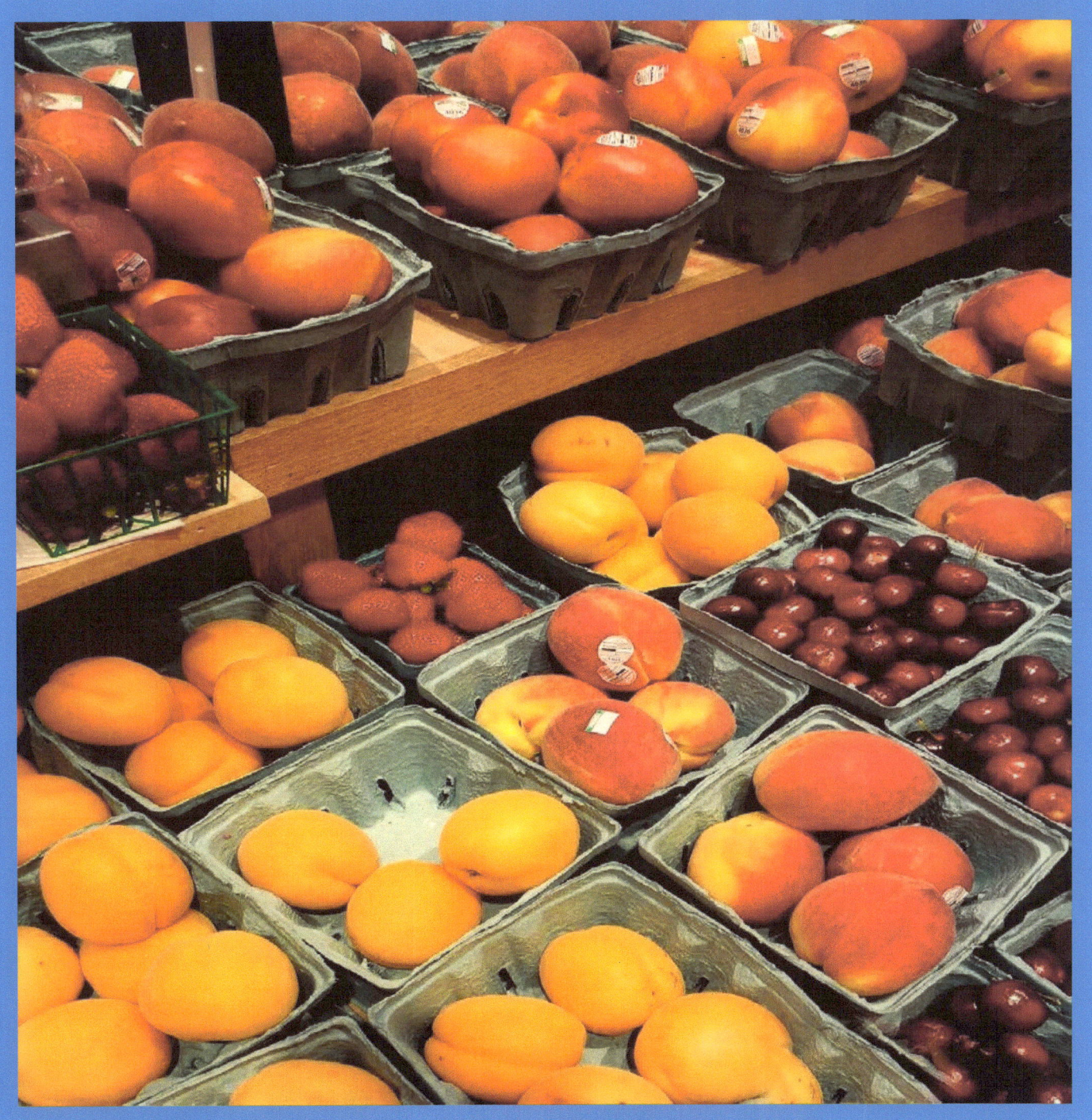

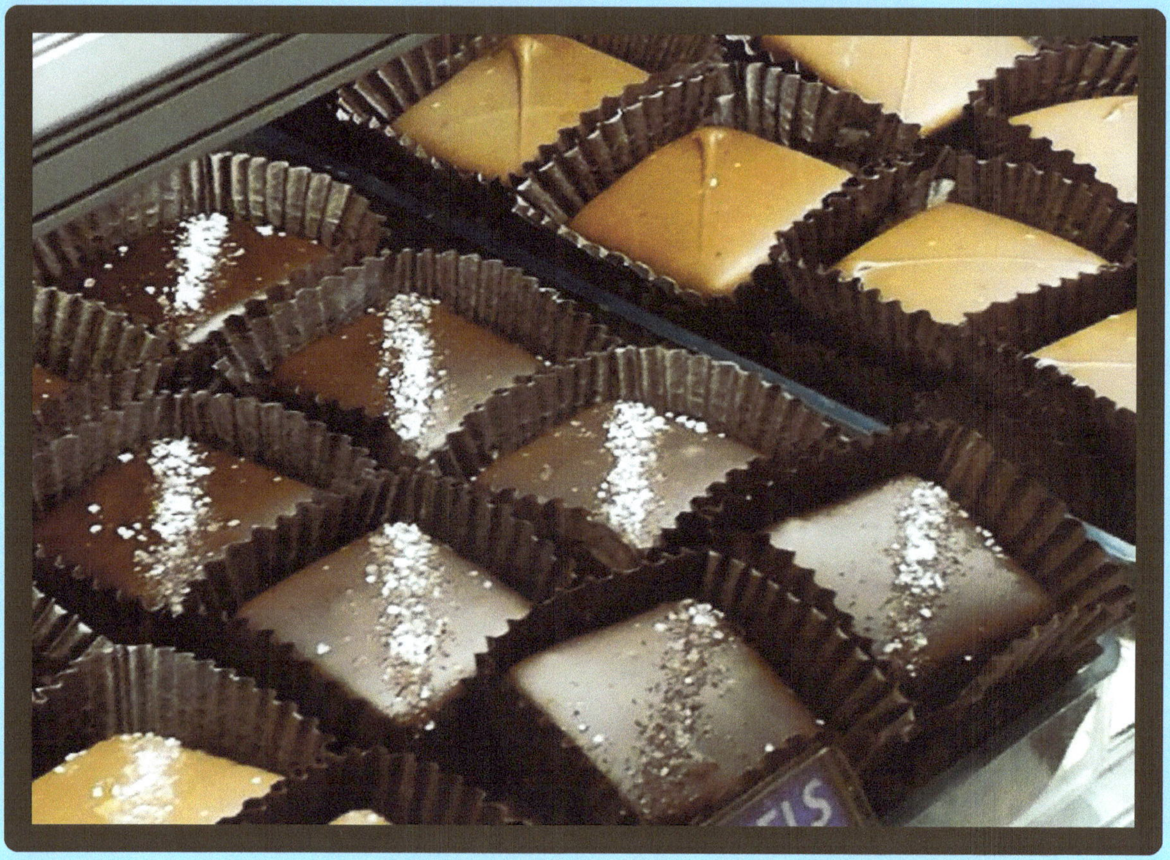

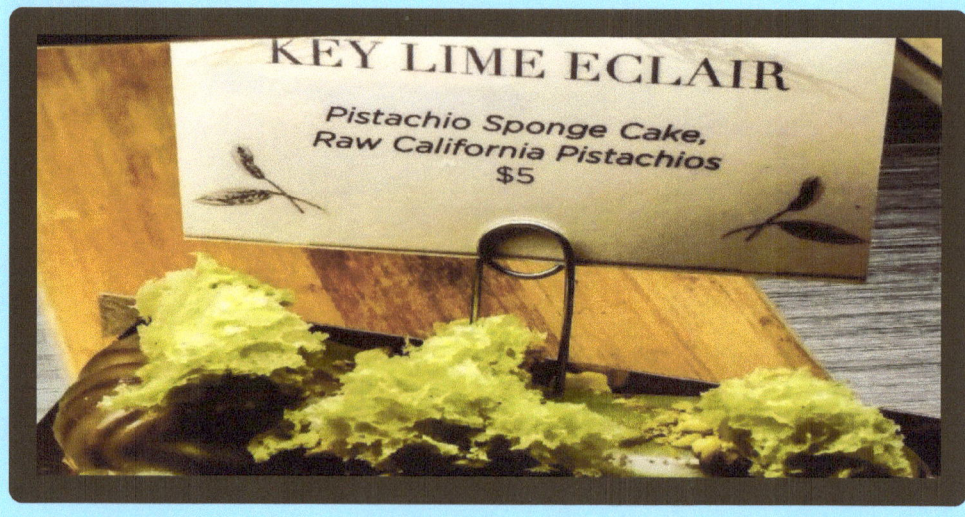

KEY LIME ECLAIR

Pistachio Sponge Cake,
Raw California Pistachios
$5

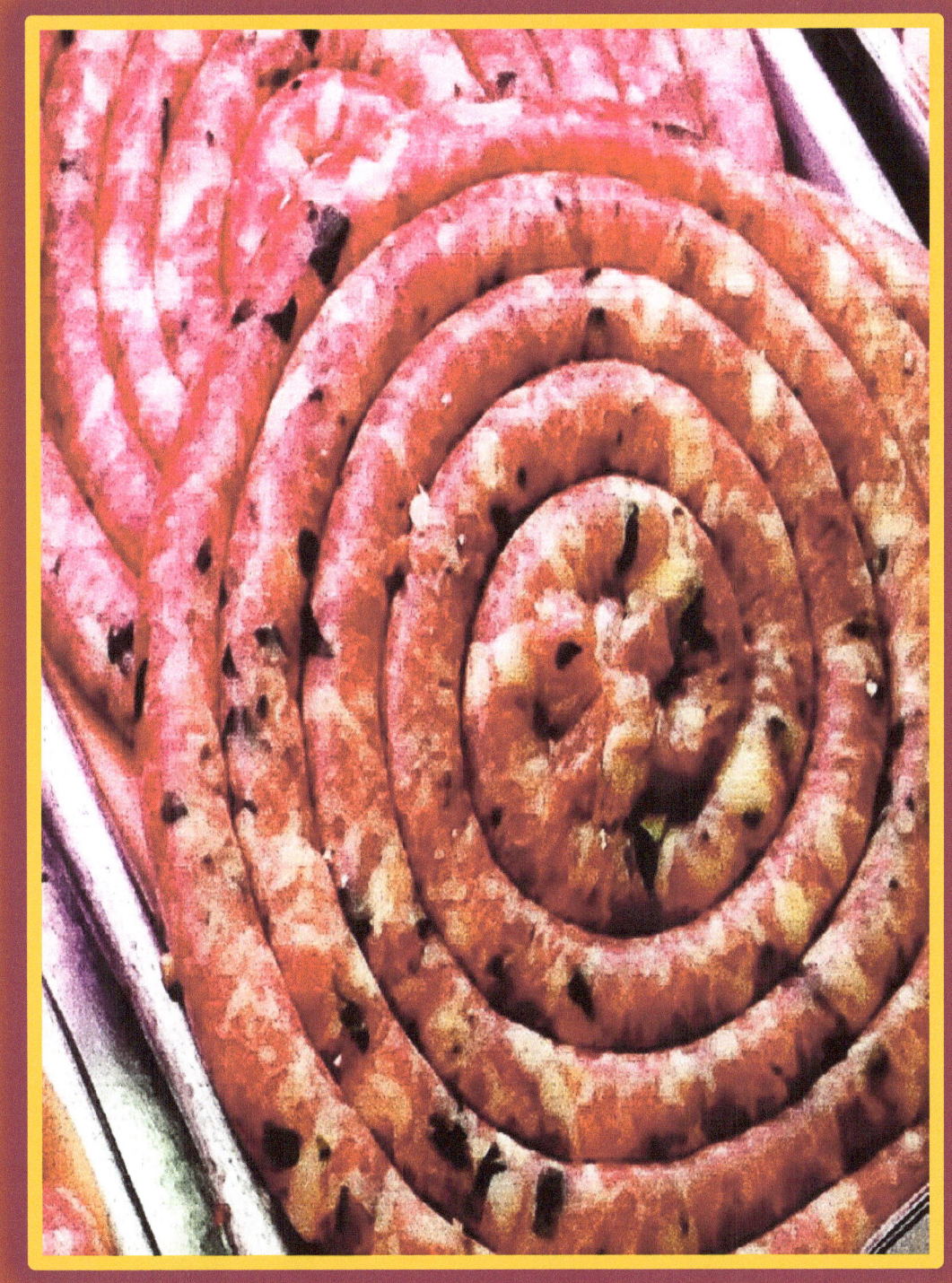

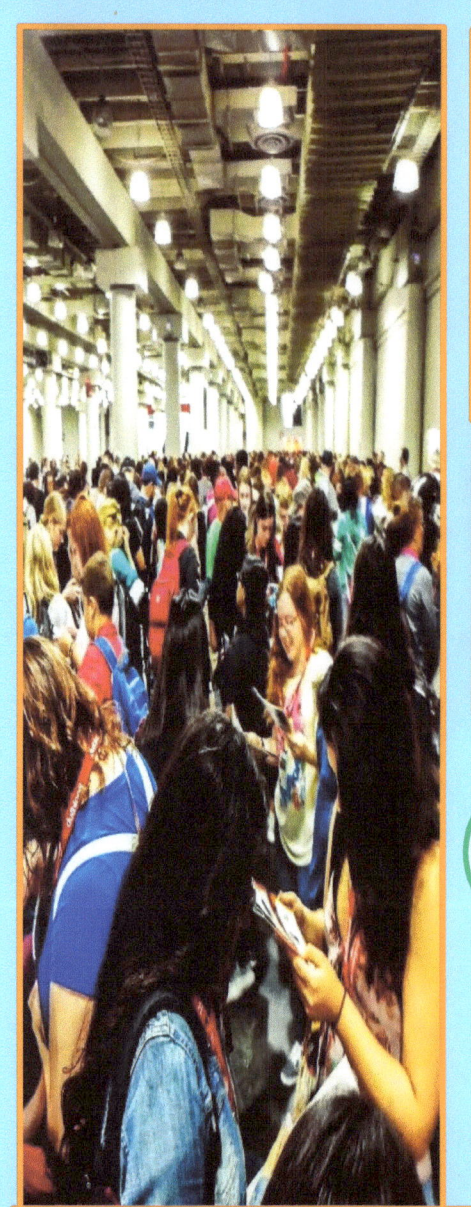

AS THE CRUSHINGLY COMPACT
AFTERNOON
IN THE CITY ENDS,
THE CABIN-DWELLER
SUDDENLY CRIES OUT:

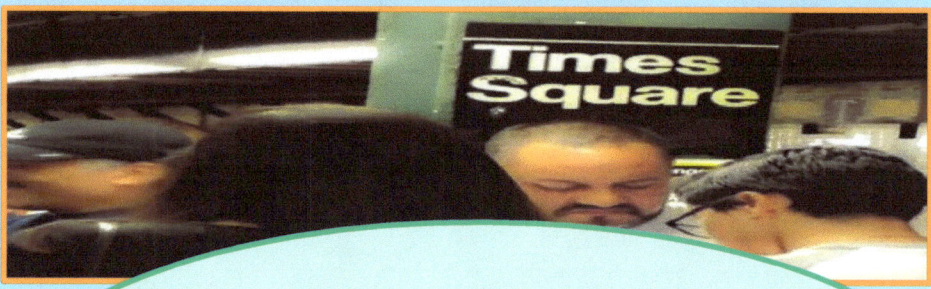

*"SUNLIGHT AND
ELBOW ROOM!*

I NEED SOME, NOW!"

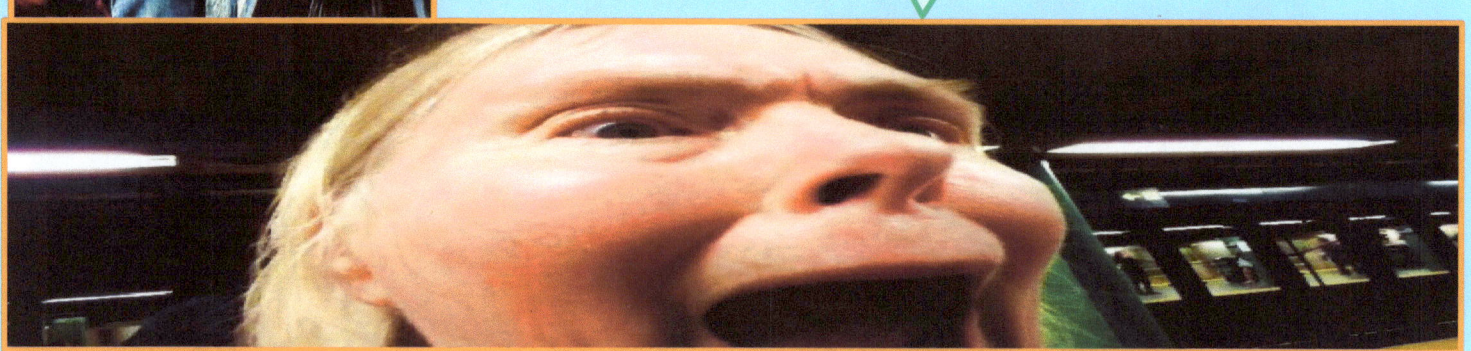

THE LONG ISLAND RAILROAD
DEPARTS NONE TOO EARLY
FOR THOSE WHO SEEK
SOME PATCH OF GREEN.

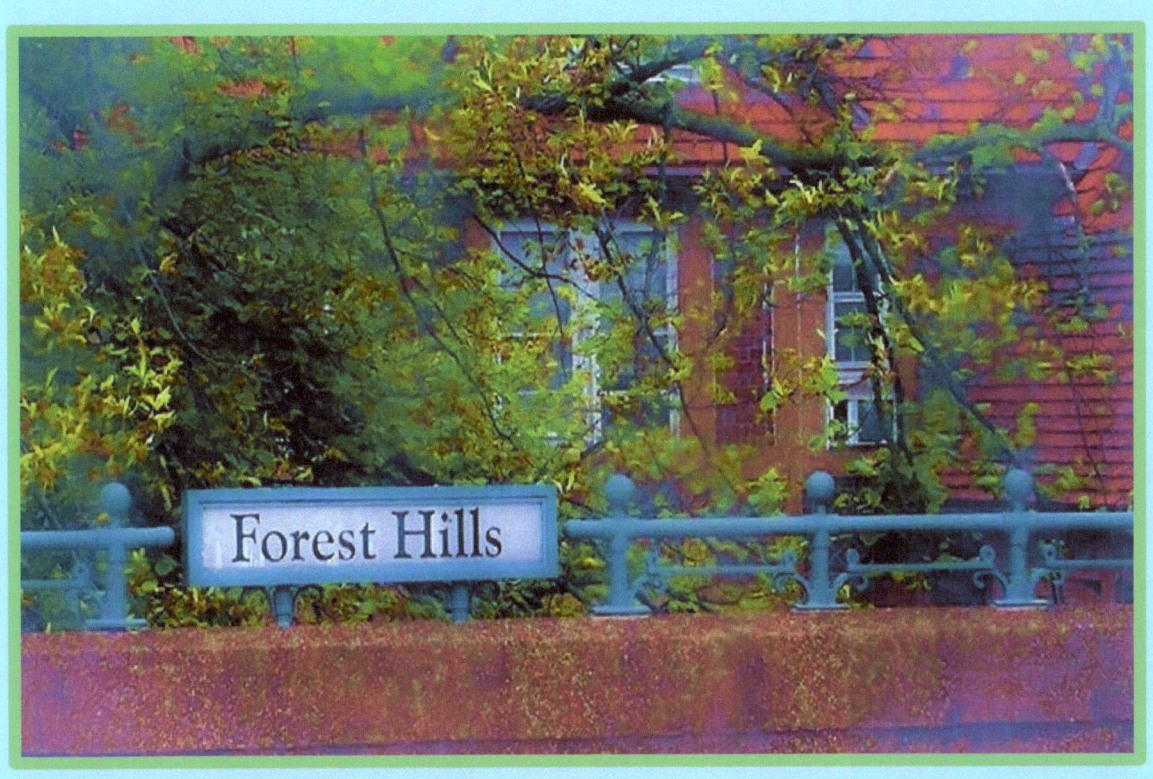

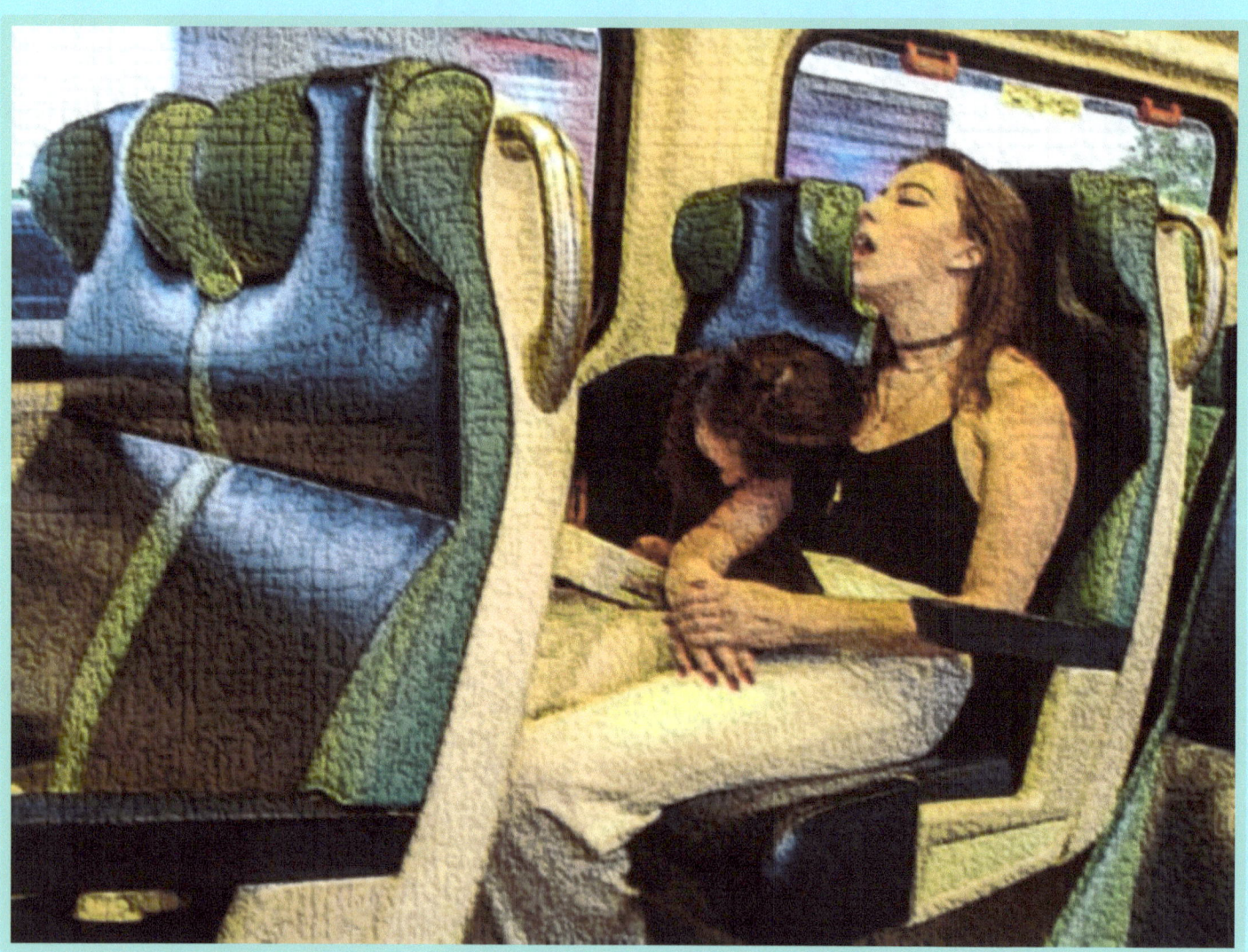

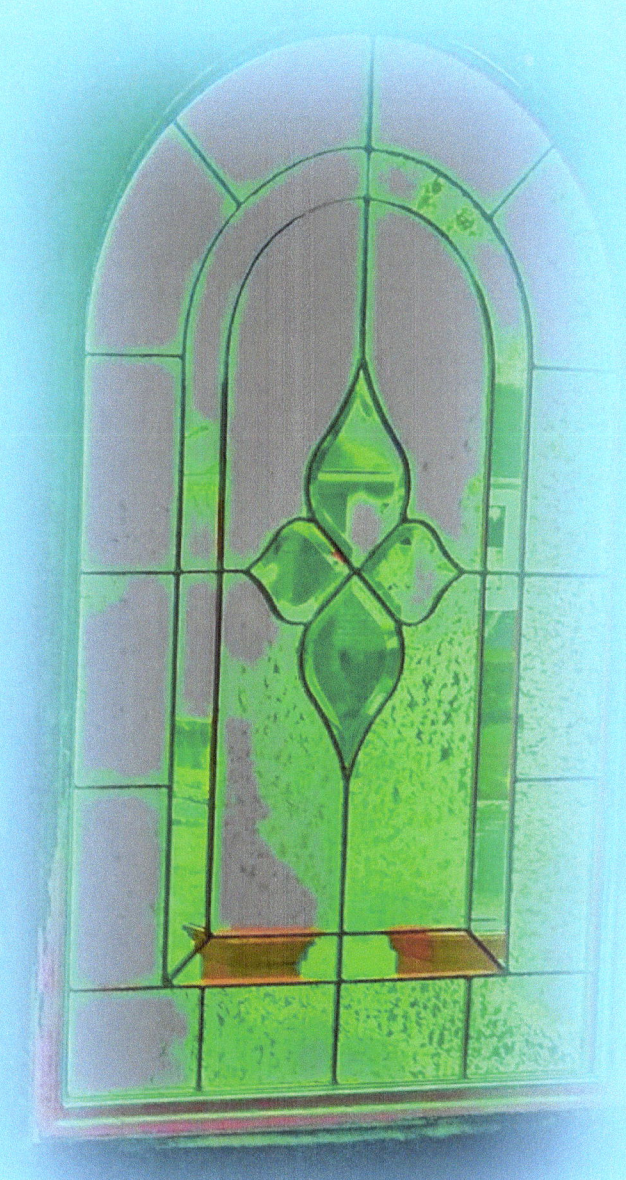

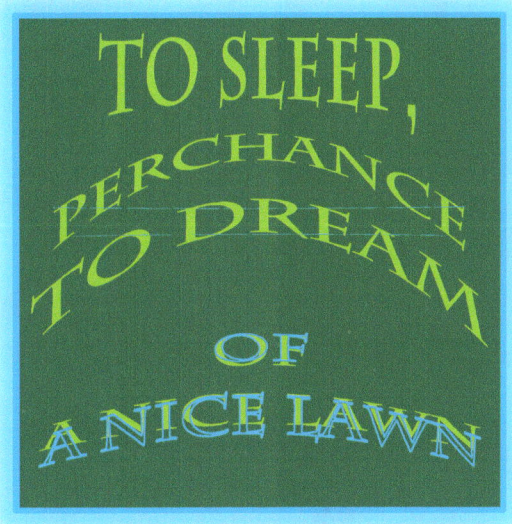

TO SLEEP,
PERCHANCE
TO DREAM
OF
A NICE LAWN

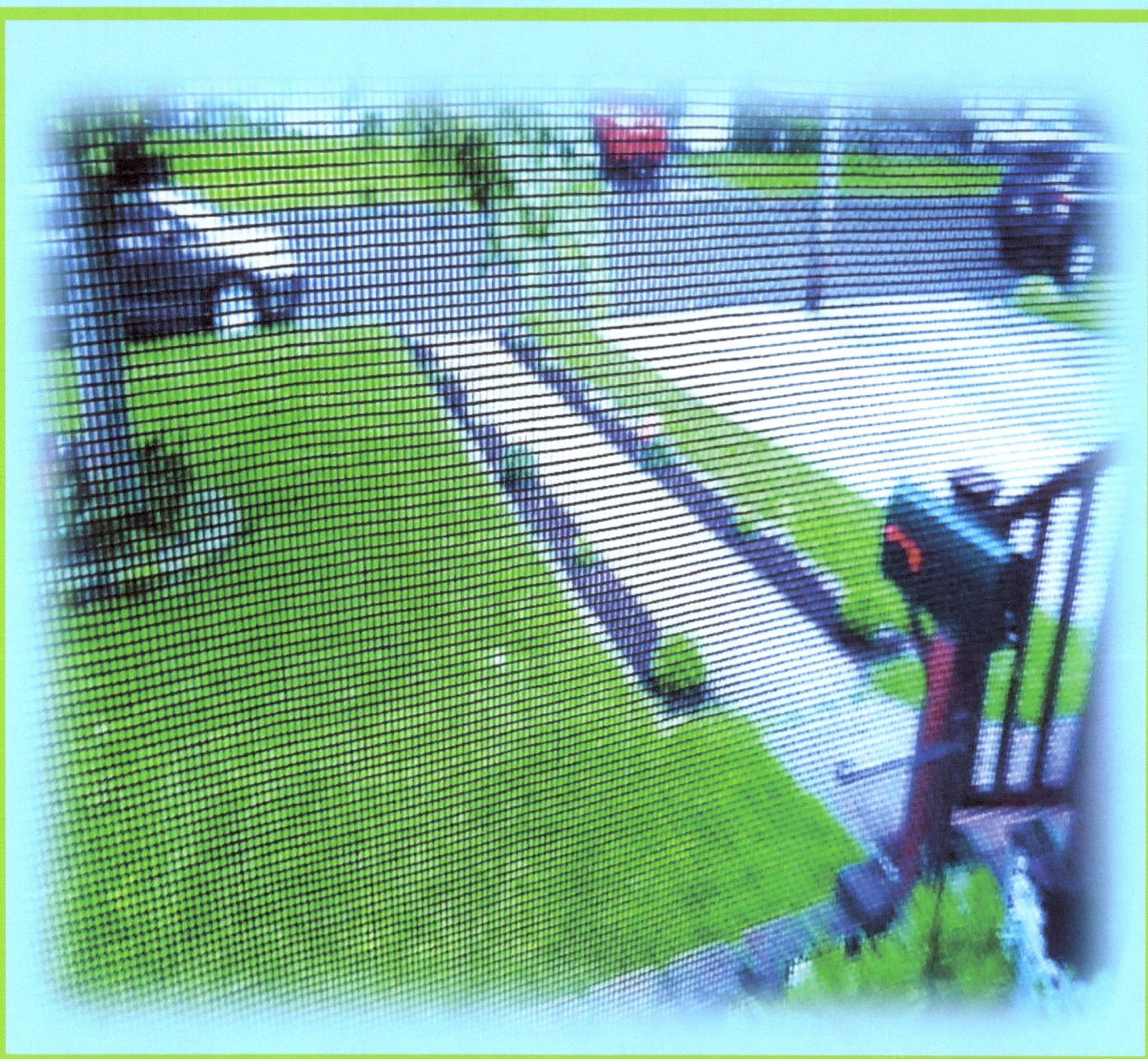

OR BETTER YET...

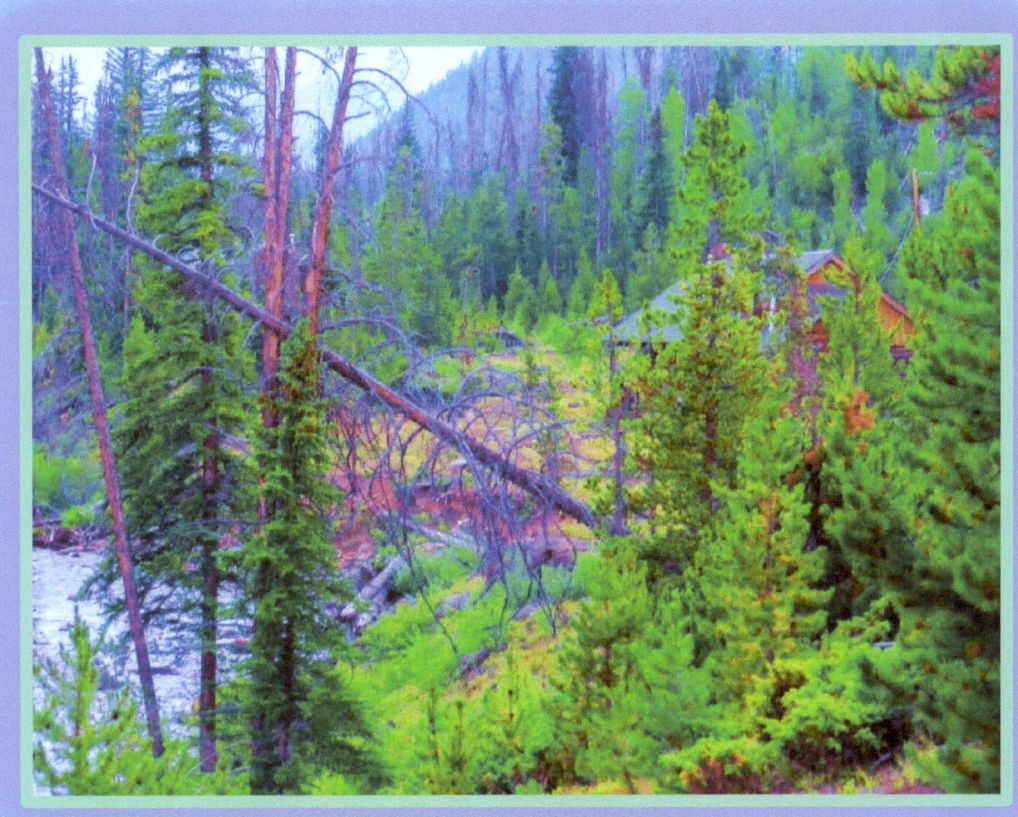

A CABIN IN THE WOODS.

Echo Hill Arts Press
is pleased to make available

Images from Atwood

A Pictorial Diversion series

for Times of Waiting

https://www.atwoodcutting.com
http://www.sleepingmoosesaga.com

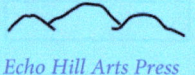

Echo Hill Arts Press